The Faith
Understood

An Introduction to Catholic Theology

The Faith Understood

An Introduction to Catholic Theology

Mark J. Zia, S.T.D.

EMMAUS
ROAD
PUBLISHING

Steubenville, Ohio
www.emmausroad.org

Emmaus Road Publishing
1468 Parkview Circle
Steubenville, Ohio 43952

Library of Congress Control Number: 2013936192
ISBN: 978-1-937155-98-8

Cover design and layout by: Theresa Westling
Cover images: The Last Supper, Lorenzo Monaco (circa 1370-1425) / Wikimedia Commons
The Four Evangelists, artist unknown (1425-1430) / Wikimedia Commons

Nihil Obstat: Leon Suprenant, *Censor Librorum*
Imprimatur: Most Reverend Joseph F. Naumann, Archbishop of Kansas City in Kansas
August 24, 2012

In memory of my infant son,
Mark Michael Zia,
who has gone to his eternal reward with the Lord.

Acknowledgments

I would like to thank several of my colleagues in the Theology Department here at Benedictine College for graciously reviewing the various chapters of this work and offering constructive criticism: Dr. Benjamin (Jamie) Blosser, Dr. John Rziha, Dr. Matthew Ramage, Dr. Richard White, Dr. Andy Swafford, and Fr. Denis Meade, O.S.B. I also wish to thank and acknowledge my assistant, Ms. Monica Kopp, for her invaluable assistance with proofreading the entirety of this manuscript, and Mr. Leon Suprenant for his editorial suggestions. Any shortcomings of this book are entirely my own.

TABLE OF CONTENTS

Introduction

The Faith Understood: An Introduction to Catholic Theology provides the reader with a solid introduction to the most significant creedal teachings of the Catholic Church. It is the first of a possible series of projected texts centered upon a better understanding of Catholicism in its various aspects, and a humble contribution to the "Year of Faith" announced by Pope Benedict XVI, beginning October 11, 2012.

For Catholics, this book will help clarify and explain central teachings of a faith that many proclaim, but relatively few sufficiently understand. For non-Catholics, this book will present what Catholics truly believe, thereby providing a platform for ecumenical discussions. This book is written in a style that constantly references authoritative sources for Catholics. The copious footnotes focus upon the Bible, the *Catechism of the Catholic Church* (hereafter referred to as "the Catechism"), the documents of the Second Vatican Council, and many other magisterial documents in order to direct the motivated reader to the sources for a more in-depth treatment of the issues presented. Indeed such a focus on both the Catechism and Vatican II is timely, since the opening of the Year of Faith on October 11th falls on the 50th anniversary of the convocation of Vatican II, as well as the 20th anniversary of the promulgation of the Catechism.

The Faith Understood

Largely structured around the first pillar (creed) of the Catechism, this book is not meant to be a substitute for the Catechism itself, but an aid to understand the richness and reasonability of the Church's major teachings. Academic, but not difficult to read, this book is ideal for college students, seminarians, adult faith formation programs, high school teachers, and anyone else who is motivated to learn more about the Catholic faith in complete faithfulness to the Church's Magisterium.

The chapters of this book are meant to be read in order, since earlier chapters will explain terms and concepts used in later chapters, thereby gradually building up the body of knowledge gained by the reader.

2

Chapter 1

Introduction to the Discipline of Theology

Overview

The term "theology" comes from two Greek words, *theos* and *logos*. Whereas the term *theos* simply means "God," the term *logos* is a bit more complex. Originally part of the philosophical heritage of classical Greek, *logos* in its basic sense may refer to a word, a deed, or a thought, but it also refers to a principle of reason, of intelligibility. The discipline of *theology*, therefore, is a reasoning process about God and all He has made known to us through a process called divine Revelation. Divine Revelation may be defined as the self-disclosure of God and His plan for our salvation. Note that divine Revelation does not simply concern God and what He has manifested to us, but it also highlights His plan for each of us. This two-fold focus of divine Revelation reflects the fact that God is not interested in simply telling us all about Himself, but He constantly invites us all to enter into living communion with Him, to share in His very Trinitarian life. Thus, the Catechism tells us:

> The Fathers of the Church distinguish between the-ology (*theologia*) and economy (*oikonomia*). "Theol-ogy" refers to the mystery of God's inmost life within the Blessed Trinity and "economy" to all the works by which God reveals himself and communicates his

life. Through the *oikonomia* the *theologia* is revealed to us; but conversely, the *theologia* illuminates the whole *oikonomia*. God's works reveal who he is in himself; the mystery of his inmost being enlightens our understanding of all his works. So it is, analogously, among human persons. A person discloses himself in his actions, and the better we know a person, the better we understand his actions. (236)

If I take a look at the fruit trees in my neighborhood, I immediately observe that many are strong with beautiful green leaves, yet I also notice a few with withering brown leaves and flimsy branches. The healthy trees will bear succulent fruit, and by the same token, the sickly trees will bear diseased fruit at best. Jesus himself uses this observation in his own teaching, "So, every sound tree bears good fruit, but the bad tree bears evil fruit. A sound tree cannot bear evil fruit, nor can a bad tree bear good fruit" (Mt. 7: 17–18). By analogy, just as the tree is known to be good by the good fruit it produces, so can God and His goodness be known through the works of his hand that are evident in the world around us. In this way, the *oikonomia* (the economy, which refers to all the wonderful things God has created) bears witness to the *theologia* (the mystery of God in Himself), just as the truth of God's Being (the *theologia*) already tells us in advance of the wonderful masterpieces of creation (the *oikonomia*) we can expect from Him.

The Bible

The Second Vatican Council teaches that "the study of the sacred page should be the very soul of sacred theology"[1] and it should be no surprise to any Christian that the Bible is a primary source for us to study theology. Defined as the inspired and inerrant written word of God, the Bible consists of God's self-communication to us for the sake of our salvation. Much more will be said about the importance

---

1 Second Vatican Council, Dogmatic Constitution on Divine Revelation *Dei Verbum* (November 18, 1965), no. 24. All citations from the Second Vatican Council are taken from Austin Flannery, *The Documents of Vatican II, Volume 1: The Conciliar and Post Conciliar Documents* (New York: Costello Publishers, 1996).

of the Bible in later chapters of this book dedicated specifically to an understanding of the Bible.

The Church Fathers

The Benedictine monk St. Anselm of Canterbury (who died in 1109) aptly defined theology as "faith seeking understanding." Persons who dedicate their lives to this study, whether these individuals are members of the clergy, religious, or the laity are called theologians. Yet those theologians whose insights are considered to be superior to the rest are the saints. Saints share in God's divine wisdom through their spiritual closeness to Him, living in a state of extraordinary virtue and holiness.[2] Whereas any intelligent person is able to learn *about* God, the saints *experience* what they learn by holiness of life and are supernaturally led into a greater understanding of God's inmost life. For this reason the Church has always strongly encouraged the readers of Scripture not simply to consult the insights and opinions of modern scholars (which are both helpful and important), but also to rediscover the wisdom of the great saints of the Church in their biblical interpretation.

Knowledge that comes through an intimate, contemplative union with God far surpasses what can be learned through purely academic pursuits. Thus one can argue that the *Story of a Soul* by St. Thérèse of Lisieux penetrates far more deeply into the truth of God than a purely intellectual work by a scholar who may be learned in things of the world, but neglects the primacy of the moral and spiritual life. Therefore we must place greater weight on the biblical commentaries, homilies, catecheses, reflections and the like offered by the great saints of the Church than those of contemporary scholars.[3]

Of these saints, those who most profoundly help us to understand our faith are the Fathers and Doctors of the Church. They are authoritative and reliable sources for studying theology, as Pope Leo XIII expressed in the following words:

> The opinion of the Fathers is also of very great weight when they treat of these matters in their capacity of

---

2   God calls everyone to be a saint; sanctity is not for the few, but it is a universal call.
3   To reiterate, contemporary scholarship is very beneficial, but it must always be organically linked to the collective wisdom that preceded it, of which the Fathers and Doctors of the Church, the liturgy, and other saints are a witness.

doctors, unofficially; not only because they excel in their knowledge of revealed doctrine and in their acquaintance with many things which are useful in understanding the apostolic Books, but because they are men of eminent sanctity and of ardent zeal for the truth, on whom God has bestowed a more ample measure of His light. Wherefore the expositor should make it his duty to follow their footsteps with all reverence, and to use their labours with intelligent appreciation.[4]

There is a distinction that can be drawn between the Fathers of the Church and the Doctors of the Church. The Fathers of the Church are those men who were orthodox in their understanding of the faith; who lived their faith in holiness; who were specifically declared by the Church to be "Fathers," and who lived within approximately the first eight centuries after Christ.[5] Doctors[6] of the Church, on the other hand, are those individuals who made significant contributions to the Church through their profound understanding of the faith, regardless of when they lived. Many Doctors of the Church are also Fathers of the Church, and a few women are also included among the ranks of the Doctors.[7] Of all the Doctors of the Church, eight stand out in particular who are also known as Fathers of the Church. They are referred to as the Great Doctors of the West (Latin speaking)—Ambrose, Jerome, Augustine, and Gregory the Great—and the Great Doctors of the East (Greek speaking)—Athanasius, Basil, Gregory Nazianzus, and John Chrysostom. We shall briefly survey the importance of these holy men, as well as suggest ways in which we who live in the 21st century can learn from their wisdom and emulate their example.

---

4 Pope Leo XIII, Encyclical Letter on the Study of Holy Scripture *Providentissimus Deus* (November 18, 1893), no. 14.

5 An "ecclesial writer" is a Christian who would otherwise be considered a "Father" if not for the fact that there was a question concerning the person's sanctity or orthodoxy. Examples of influential ecclesial writers include Origen and Tertullian.

6 From the Latin *docere*, meaning "to teach," a doctor is one who teaches.

7 Saints Teresa of Avila, Catherine of Siena, Thérèse of Lisieux, and more recently (October of 2012) Hildegard of Bingen.

THE FOUR GREAT DOCTORS OF THE WEST

Treating them in chronological order, the first Great Doctor of the West is St. Ambrose, who died about 397. He was bishop of Milan, Italy, and strongly defended the autonomy of the Church against unjust intervention by secular authorities. It was the power of the Holy Spirit working through his preaching that resulted in the conversion of St. Augustine to the faith. From St. Ambrose we learn the power of the preached word of God. It may be helpful here to consider the biblical teaching that the Gospel is "the power of God for salvation," as taught by St. Paul in Romans 1:16. The Greek term *dunamis* is translated as "power," which entered the English language as "dynamite." Indeed the preached word of God is "dynamite" for the Christian seeking to make Christ known in the world! We also learn from St. Ambrose the importance of putting the demands of our faith before those of politics, a mature decision that may frequently result in political unpopularity, but also renewed spiritual strength.

The second Great Doctor of the West is St. Jerome, who died in 420. He was a contemporary of St. Augustine and was known for his zeal in defending and explaining the faith. His greatest accomplishment was the translation of the entire Bible into Latin, which is known as the Vulgate. St. Jerome was a witness to the importance of the Bible as a privileged vehicle for us to come to know Jesus, demonstrating unshakable zeal for the faith. Pope Benedict XVI offers the following reflection on St. Jerome: "What can we learn from St. Jerome? It seems to me, this above all: to love the Word of God in Sacred Scripture. St. Jerome said: 'Ignorance of the Scriptures is ignorance of Christ.' It is therefore important that every Christian live in contact and in personal dialogue with the Word of God given to us in Sacred Scripture."[8] It is significant that this famous saying of St. Jerome has its origins in St. Jerome's commentary on the Book of Isaiah. This fact helps us to understand that all of the Bible, and not just the New Testament, is inspired by God and therefore profitable in helping us to learn about Christ. Indeed throughout the Old Testament the mystery of Christ was already hidden until its proper revelation at the time of His coming through the Incarnation.

---

8   Pope Benedict XVI, General Audience of November 7, 2007.

The third Great Doctor of the West is St. Augustine, bishop of Hippo, who died about the year 430. He left the greatest number of written works of any individual Father of the Church and is regarded as the greatest of the Fathers.[9] Prior to his conversion, Augustine lived a wild, godless life, even fathering a son named Adeodatus outside of marriage. Through the persistent prayers of his mother, St. Monica, Augustine was finally converted to the faith when he was in his early thirties. Augustine produced "the first great synthesis of philosophy and theology, embracing currents of thought both Greek and Latin. In him too the great unity of knowledge, grounded in the thought of the Bible, was both confirmed and sustained by a depth of speculative thinking."[10] His autobiography is called the *Confessions*, a title that emphasizes praise of God, as well as penitence over his sinful past.[11] His most famous quote is found in the opening paragraph of this autobiography: "Our hearts are restless, O Lord, until they rest in thee."[12] From St. Augustine we learn that it is never too late to repent of our sins and return to Christ, and we witness the power of intercessory prayer as shown through St. Monica.[13] Additionally, we all can appreciate the truth in Augustine's observation that we all seek God by nature, and only He can truly satisfy the deepest aspirations of the human heart.

The fourth and final Great Doctor of the West is Pope St. Gregory the Great, who died about 604. He was a monk who later became the first Benedictine[14] to be elected pope, and went on to become one of the very few popes in history who received the title "the Great."[15] The Gregorian chant is named after him, and he originated one of the most eloquent titles for the pope as *servus servorum Dei*, "the servant of the servants of God." Reflecting on this title, Pope Benedict XVI comments: "Coined by him, this phrase was not just a pious formula

---

9 See Pope Benedict XVI, General Audience of January 9, 2008.
10 Pope John Paul II, Encyclical Letter on Faith and Reason *Fides et ratio* (September 14, 1998), no. 40.
11 See Pope Benedict XVI, General Audience of February 20, 2008.
12 St. Augustine, first paragraph of *Confessions*.
13 "The prayer of a righteous man has great power in its effects" (Jas. 5:16).
14 Religious Order founded by St. Benedict (d. 543), the founder of Western monasticism.
15 Other popes known as "the Great" include Pope Leo I, and by some accounts, Pope Nicholas I. It is very possible that the late John Paul II may also one day be known as "the Great," a title that originates with the people rather than officially by the Church.

on his lips but a true manifestation of his way of living and acting. He was immediately struck by the humility of God, who in Christ made himself our servant. He washed and [still] washes our dirty feet."[16] How magnificent was this man's humility, that rather than view the office of the papacy as an institution of power, he was completely mindful of his own frailty. From St. Gregory the Great we truly learn the importance of humility in the Christian life. We are also reminded that the beauty of the sacred liturgy is rooted in its celebration of God, instead of the modern temptation to reduce the sacred liturgy to a celebration of our own innovations and creativity. As Pope Benedict remarked as the former Cardinal Prefect of the Congregation for the Doctrine of the Faith, "The greatness of the liturgy depends—we shall have to repeat this frequently—on its unspontaneity."[17]

THE FOUR GREAT DOCTORS OF THE EAST

In addition to the four Great Doctors of the West, the Catholic Church also recognizes four Great Doctors of the East. The first is St. Athanasius, bishop of Alexandria, Egypt, who died about 373. He was exiled many times by his enemies due to his orthodox[18] views, especially for his strong defense of the full divinity of Jesus Christ in the face of the Arian heresy.[19] Yet through his numerous exiles, he was able to introduce monasticism to the West, thereby showing that God is so powerful that He can bring good even out of evil. It would have been easy for him, humanly speaking, to have been less insistent on maintaining and teaching the true faith, and to turn a blind eye to the false teachings that were being spread at his time. Yet he took his faith so seriously that he was prepared to endure any punishment inflicted on him by his enemies for his unswerving witness to the full truth of Christianity. From St. Athanasius' example, we are encouraged to defend our faith against those who attack it, and to trust God in all times, especially in times of darkness and difficulty. As Christians,

---

16 Pope Benedict XVI, General Audience of June 4, 2008.

17 Joseph Ratzinger, *The Spirit of the Liturgy* (Ignatius Press: San Francisco, 2000), 166.

18 Here the term "orthodox" refers to correct theological views, whereas "unorthodox" refers to unacceptable theological views.

19 As will be discussed in chapter eight, the Arians denied the true divinity of Jesus Christ, believing that He was a creature.

we are followers of Christ, so just as our Lord was persecuted and ultimately put to death for His teachings, we as His followers should not be surprised if we are persecuted in our lives. Rather than live in fear and compromise, let us live according to the exhortation of St. Peter: "Always be prepared to make a defense to any one who calls you to account for the hope that is in you, yet do it with gentleness and reverence" (1 Pet. 3:15).

The second Great Doctor of the East is St. Basil, bishop of Caesarea and the brother of St. Gregory of Nyssa. St. Basil, who died about 379, was known as "a practical man, totally dedicated to the service of the Church in a position of responsibility and authority,"[20] and he is considered the Father of Eastern Monasticism. He strongly preferred the lifestyle of monks living together as a community instead of the older model of monks who lived in solitude,[21] and from St. Basil we learn the importance of community life and of growing in holiness as a community. Although the vast majority of us do not and will not make a monastic profession, as human persons we are called to live in communion with others in society. St. Basil reminds us of the downfalls of individualism; the importance of cherishing life with others; and the necessity of "attentive, critical and creative participation in today's culture."[22]

The third Great Doctor of the East is St. Gregory Nazianzus, who died about 389. He was the archbishop of Constantinople and known as "the Theologian" for his eloquent defense of the faith as found in his *Theological Orations*.[23] In order to promote peace within his region, he resigned as archbishop, and is well-remembered for his most famous quote regarding the full significance of the Incarnation: "What has not been assumed[24] has not been healed." From St. Gregory Nazianzus we learn the importance of considering the good of others, and not merely

---

20 Jordan Aumann, *Christian Spirituality in the Catholic Tradition* (San Francisco: Ignatius Press, 1985), 44.

21 The monastic lifestyle characterized by monks living together in community is called the cenobitic life, whereas the monastic lifestyle characterized by monks living individually in isolation from others is called eremitical life.

22 Pope Benedict XVI, General Audience of August 1, 2007.

23 Pope Benedict XVI, General Audience of August 8, 2007.

24 The Word of God "assumed" or "took upon Himself" a full, true human nature at the Incarnation.

our own good, and how important it is for Christians to defend the full truth of the Incarnation against those who deny or attempt to diminish it. The final Great Doctor of the East is St. John Chrysostom, who died in 407. He was Patriarch of Constantinople and has a Byzantine liturgy named after him. His preaching was so superb that he was called "Chrysostom," which was not a formal part of his name, but a term that means "golden-mouthed." He was exiled because of his orthodoxy and died before he arrived at his place of exile. St. John's example reminds us that if we remain faithful to Jesus, we can expect to be persecuted, as stated by St. Paul: "Indeed all who desire to live a godly life in Christ Jesus will be persecuted. . ." (2 Tim. 3:12). Yet we must have hope in the Lord, remaining steadfast to the end, at which time the Lord will crown us with victory. Just as St. John's written works "cross the whole globe like flashes of lightening,"[25] so too are we called to be a light to the world through heroically living our faith.

The Magisterium

Whereas the collective writings of the Fathers and Doctors of the Church are one way by which we can access the rich Tradition of the Church, the most direct, ever-present guide available to us for studying theology is the Magisterium of the Church. A *magister* (masculine) or *magistra* (feminine) is a teacher, and the Magisterium may be defined as the official teaching authority of the Church, consisting of the pope and bishops who are in union with him. Every pope, sometimes referred to as the Supreme Pontiff or the Vicar of Christ, is the successor of St. Peter and visible head of the Church, whose primary duties are to protect, interpret, and pass down the teachings of Christ in their full purity. Through various means, including encyclicals, homilies, and catechetical addresses, the pope spiritually nourishes the People of God, according to the mandate Jesus gave to Peter, "feed my sheep" (Jn. 21:15–17).

In addition to methods by which the pope teaches his flock directly, the pope may summon a world-wide gathering of all Catholic bishops to discuss issues pertinent to the Church and the Christian life in a

---

25 An anonymous copyist, cited by Pope Benedict XVI in his General Address of September 19, 2007.

collegial manner. The last time this was done was the convocation of the Second Vatican Council by Pope John XXIII, which took place from 1962 to 1965. On average there is one such council, called a General or Ecumenical Council, every one hundred years, with a total of twenty-one held to date. Although the early councils of the Church were not always summoned by the pope (but rather by the emperor), it is important to realize that in order for a council to be recognized as truly authoritative, it must receive recognition by the pope, since the bishops who compose the council have no binding authority unless united with the pope. More shall be said about the Magisterium in chapter five.

A particularly recent and indispensable product of the Church's Magisterium is the Catechism, which was begun in 1987 and ultimately approved by Pope John Paul II in 1992, representing the breadth and richness of the entire Catholic Church, both in the East and in the West. A "catechism" is simply a manual for theological instruction, and there have been (and will be) many catechisms in the Church's history, some authored by individuals, others by Bishops' Conferences, yet only two by the Universal Church. Of these two universal catechisms, the *Catechism of the Council of Trent* (written in the 16th century) was addressed to priests and bishops, whereas the *Catechism of the Catholic Church* is addressed to all persons. Like the *Catechism of the Council of Trent* that came four hundred years before it, the *Catechism of the Catholic Church* is the only other catechism issued to the entire Church, with the full weight of the Magisterium behind it:

> The *Catechism of the Catholic Church*, which I approved 25 June last and the publication of which I today order by virtue of my Apostolic Authority, is a statement of the Church's faith and of Catholic doctrine, attested to or illumined by Sacred Scripture, Apostolic Tradition and the Church's Magisterium. I declare it to be a valid and legitimate instrument for ecclesial communion and a sure norm for teaching the faith.[26]

---

26 Pope John Paul II, Apostolic Constitution on the Publication of the Catechism of the Catholic Church *Fidei depositum* (October 11, 1992), IV.

Pope Benedict XVI echoes this assessment in stating, "In order to arrive at a systematic knowledge of the content of the faith, all can find in the *Catechism of the Catholic Church* a precious and indispensable tool. It is one of the most important fruits of the Second Vatican Council."[27] It must be stressed that since this Catechism was promulgated by Pope John Paul II for the Universal Church, it has the highest level of the Church's ordinary teaching authority. This fact means that all other theological claims and teachings are to be judged by how well they harmonize with the Catechism, and should a contradiction be found between the two, the Catechism is to be accepted as correct. Accordingly, the value of this one volume is immense for all Catholics who wish to learn more about their faith, as well as for non-Catholics who would like a candid understanding of what the Catholic Church actually teaches, without having to resort to speculation and misunderstandings that tend to abound concerning theological matters.

Given its importance for accurately understanding Catholic theology, we shall refer to the Catechism using the abbreviation "CCC" in the parenthetical notation in text and the footnotes. All references to the Catechism are always made using numbers corresponding to the bold-print paragraph numbers instead of the page numbers. This practice ensures that everyone is literally "on the same page," whether persons are reading the Catechism in English, Spanish, or Chinese, and irrespective of whether they are consulting standard print, large print, or electronic editions.[28]

The Catechism is divided into four "pillars," with the sequence of their appearance very instructive. The first pillar is that of Creed, signifying that the starting point for theology is our faith in God. The second pillar is Cult. Although the term 'cult' tends to suggest something negative, it simply comes from the Latin term *cultus* meaning "worship," and it pertains to the sacramental economy of the Church. The faith that we profess (pillar 1) is now nourished through acts of worship (pillar 2), which find both their source and summit in the

---

27 Pope Benedict XVI, Apostolic Letter for the Indication of the Year of Faith *Porta fidei* (October 11, 2011), no. 11.

28 In addition to the standard book format of the CCC, keep in mind that the whole resource is also available online on the Vatican website (www.vatican.va) under the "resource library" area.

sacramental life of the Church. The third pillar is the Commandments. Only after we have been spiritually nourished through the sacraments do we receive the supernatural graces needed to persevere in charity and to keep all of God's commandments. Finally, in keeping the commandments (pillar 3), we advance in our relationship with God, which is realized in prayer. Prayer is the fourth and final pillar of the Catechism, and refers to our dialogue and communion with God. Expressing these same concepts in another way, John Paul II writes:

> The four parts are related one to the other: the Christian mystery is the object of faith (first part); it is celebrated and communicated in liturgical actions (second part); it is present to enlighten and sustain the children of God in their actions (third part); it is the basis for our prayer, the privileged expression of which is the *Our Father*, and it represents the object of our supplication, our praise and our intercession (fourth part).[29]

The Catechism includes some useful navigational aids:

- Numbers found within the margins of the Catechism indicate cross-referenced paragraphs which are devoted to the same topic.
- Footnotes will primarily indicate biblical references, and the text in small print often offers insights from the saints and the Tradition of the Church.
- The "In brief" sections give a summary of the primary points contained within that section, and indices at the end indicate further cross-referenced material.
- Some editions include a comprehensive index of citations to indicate where the Catechism quotes other sources, such as Canon Law, Scripture, and the Documents of Vatican II, and some editions contain a helpful glossary as well.

---

29 Pope John Paul II, *Fidei depositum*, III.

Conclusion

The testimony of Sacred Scripture combined with the profound theological insights of the Fathers of the Church, Doctors of the Church, and other saints are highly beneficial and authoritative sources for studying theology. With the guidance of the Magisterium, we are able to discern the proper way to interpret these ancient witnesses who continue to speak to every age through their writings and through the liturgical celebrations of the Church, which is the most natural way for the theological beliefs of the People of God to be passed down from one generation to the next.

Chapter 2

The Relationship between Faith and Reason

Overview

The ecclesiastical writer Tertullian (who died approximately 230) asked an extremely penetrating question: "What does Athens have to do with Jerusalem?" He was asking what Athens, which represented philosophy, pure reason, and nature, had in common with Jerusalem, which represented theology, faith, and grace. Today more than ever, there often tends to be two competing viewpoints regarding the relationship between faith and reason, claiming that we must accept either science or faith; that we must trust either the power of pure reason, or the spiritual illumination that comes through faith. If we apply this tension to current religious-based universities, we inevitably observe that there are some students who think that they must disavow all religious convictions before entering the biology classroom, and other students who maintain that we must cast aside all of our scientific knowledge when we enter into the theology classroom. But this situation amounts to a false dilemma.

The proper attitude towards this apparent tension is the realization that the Christian accepts all that is true in any discipline, without a need for mental subterfuge. We accept science as well as theology, reason as well as faith, the natural as well as the supernatural. The reason for this conclusion is quite simple, as St. Thomas Aquinas has reminded us: there cannot be any real discrepancy between faith and reason, because the light of both faith and reason comes from the same source, namely, God himself.[1] This observation enabled St. Augustine to say many centuries before Aquinas, "I believe, in order to understand; and I understand, the better to believe."[2] Faith indeed presupposes reason and builds upon it.

Faith

There are several ways to correctly define "faith." A biblical definition of faith is found in the Letter to the Hebrews: "Faith is the assurance of things hoped for, the conviction of things not seen" (Heb. 11:1). We supplement his biblical definition with a dogmatic one: faith is a gift of God and human act by which we completely submit our intellect and will to God. To these two definitions we can add a third, "common sense" definition of faith as the act of having complete trust and confidence in someone.[3] From these three definitions that approach the reality of faith from a different perspective, we observe that (1) faith has its origin in almighty God as one of the three infused theological virtues;[4] (2) it is directed back to God; and (3) it is a type of knowledge. We also note that faith is not simply a gift from above, but it is also a human act. It is not enough for God to give the gift; but we must freely cultivate the gift and choose to use it.

Because the proper object of faith is God Himself and the truths that He has revealed, knowledge gained through faith is more certain than knowledge gained through the scientific method.[5] Through the scientific method, we acquire new knowledge by figuring out the

---

1   See CCC 159.

2   See CCC 158.

3   Consider that only in a loose sense do we speak about having faith in another human being. "As personal adherence to God and assent to his truth, Christian faith differs from our faith in any human person. It is right and just to entrust oneself wholly to God and to believe absolutely what he says. It would be futile and false to place such faith in a creature" (CCC 150).

4   A virtue is traditionally understood as a habitual and firm disposition to do the good (see CCC 1803). Like the theological virtues of hope and charity, and unlike the cardinal virtues of prudence, justice, temperance and fortitude, the theological virtue of faith cannot be acquired through our own effort, but first must be given to us by God (see CCC 1813).

5   See CCC 157.

reasonability of the thing to be known through using our senses of sight, hearing, touch, smell and taste. Knowledge gained through reason, therefore, is "figured out" to be true. Through the knowledge that comes by faith, however, we do not acknowledge something to be true because we empirically "figured it out," but rather because God revealed it to us and we trust His authority. Whereas we can misinterpret data, have faulty sense perceptions (for example, when one is sick), and make errors in our judgments, there can be no such error on the part of God in disclosing truth to us. For this reason, knowledge revealed directly by God (which we call divine Revelation) is more certain than knowledge that we gain through mere human experience.

Two human persons of biblical history who stand out more than any others as exemplars of unconditional faith in God are Abraham and Mary. Abraham, the Patriarch of the Old Testament, is recognized by the three monotheistic religions of the world as being their father in faith.[6] Even in our own Roman Catholic liturgical tradition, there is an explicit mention of "Abraham, our father in faith" made in the Roman Canon.[7] In obedience to God, Abraham left his land and fortune, uprooting his family, and journeyed to the unknown land to which God called him. Ultimately, the depth of Abraham's faith was shown through his compliance to God's command that he slay his only son and heir, Isaac, so that the boy could be offered up to God as a sacrifice. Think of how immense his love was for his own flesh and blood, and yet he still loved God even more! How many of us today have such unconditional faith in God? In reward for his great faith, God prevented the actual sacrifice and abundantly blessed Abraham and his descendants.[8]

The second human person in salvation history who most perfectly shows forth the theological virtue of faith is Mary, the Mother of God, who submitted her entire being to God so completely that she became the living tabernacle of the Most High, from whom was born the Incarnate Son of God.[9] As great as Abraham's witness of faith truly was,

---

6   The three monotheistic religions are the three world religions that profess faith in the one God. They are Judaism, Christianity, and Islam.
7   The Roman Canon is also known as "Eucharistic Prayer I."
8   The account of this powerful event testing Abraham's faith can be found in Genesis 22:1–19.
9   See CCC 146–149.

Mary did not simply have a few tests of faith throughout her lifetime, but her entire life was mysteriously lived in absolute faith from one day to the next, formally beginning with the miraculous conception of Jesus in her womb and extending through His death, Resurrection, Ascension and beyond. On Mary's faith, consider the reflection of Pope Benedict XVI:

> The human reality created through the word finds its most perfect image in Mary's obedient faith. From the Annunciation to Pentecost she appears as a woman completely open to the will of God. She is the Immaculate Conception, the one whom God made "full of grace" (cf. Lk. 1:28) and unconditionally docile to his word (cf. Lk. 1:38). Her obedient faith shapes her life at every moment before God's plan. A Virgin ever attentive to God's word, she lives completely attuned to that word; she treasures in her heart the events of her Son, piecing them together as if in a single mosaic (cf. Lk. 2:19,51).[10]

Reflecting on the examples of Abraham and Mary, one may be tempted to think that believing in God was fine for them back in biblical days, but the importance of faith in contemporary society has lost its relevance. Is it really reasonable for a person living in the 21st century of scientific progress, cutting-edge technology, and "free thinking" to profess faith in God?

Consider the following scenario: you are walking across the street late at night when a car spins out of control and hits you, resulting in your immediate need to get to the emergency room. Once you arrive, the attending surgeon tells you that you are seriously injured and that he must operate in order for you to recover. How would you respond? Would you ask to see the surgeon's medical school transcripts, diploma, and list of references whom you can call at one o'clock in the morning, or would you eagerly consent to the operation without reservation, entrusting your life to a doctor whom you may never have even met before? If we would not think twice about trusting a complete stranger

---

10 Pope Benedict XVI, Apostolic Exhortation on the Word of God *Verbum Domini* (September 30, 2010), no. 27.

to operate on us in a potential life-and-death scenario, how much more reasonable is it to have absolute trust in our loving God, Creator and sustainer of all life! This absolute trust that has God as its proper object is called faith, and not only is it eminently reasonable to have such faith, it becomes blatantly unreasonable to refuse it.

Reason

Given what has been said, one might rashly conclude that as long as we possess faith, then we have no need for pure reason. Indeed, persons known as fideists[11] maintain such a view. Fideists claim that human reason is utterly depraved due to sin and remains utterly useless with respect to our understanding of the supernatural realm. This elevation of faith to the point of rejection of the power of reason is an error. Even the truth of the very existence of God is a datum that the human person can know through reason alone without even having faith! Consider the following solemn teaching of the First Vatican Council: "The same Holy Mother Church holds and teaches that God, the beginning and end of all things, can be known with certainty from the things that were created through the natural light of human reason. . ."[12] This teaching is explicitly taught in the New Testament by St. Paul who wrote,

> For the wrath of God is revealed from heaven against all ungodliness and wickedness of men who by their wickedness suppress the truth. For what can be known about God is plain to them, because God has shown it to them. Ever since the creation of the world his invisible nature, namely, his eternal power and deity, has been clearly perceived in the things that have been made. So they are without excuse. . . (Rom. 1:18–20)

And lest one fall into the error of thinking that this natural knowability of God is a Christian "invention," it may be helpful to consider that the same teaching is found in the Old Testament Book of

---

11 *Fides* in Latin means "faith."
12 Heinrich Denzinger, *Compendium of Creeds, Definitions, and Declarations on Matters of Faith and Morals*, trans. Peter Hünermann (San Francisco: Ignatius Press, 2012), 3004. See also CCC 36.

Wisdom, attributed to King Solomon who reigned approximately one thousand years before the advent of Christianity. This book, possibly a main source for St. Paul's teaching on this matter, states,

> For all men who were ignorant of God were foolish by nature; and they were unable from the good things that are seen to know him who exists, nor did they recognize the craftsman while paying heed to his works; but they supposed that either fire or wind or swift air, or the circle of the stars, or turbulent water, or the luminaries of heaven were the gods that rule the world. If through delight in the beauty of these things men assumed them to be gods, let them know how much better than these is their Lord, for the author of beauty created them. And if men were amazed at their power and working, let them perceive from them how much more powerful is he who formed them. For from the greatness and beauty of created things comes a corresponding perception of their Creator. (Wis. 13:1–5)

What are some examples of "evidence" of God's existence that are accessible to pure reason? Two examples readily come to mind by reflecting upon the world in which we live.[13] First, we speak of the example from contingency,[14] which can be summarized in the following manner: We instinctively know that it is better to exist than not to exist. Simply reflect upon the sheer volumes of products that are advertized and sold that enable us to live healthier and longer, and consider the number of medical procedures that are carried out with the hope of saving or prolonging the life of someone approaching death. If we had the power of life within us, we would make sure that we would not die, but we do not have such a power because we are contingent beings, that is, we are utterly dependant on a higher power for our continued survival. Yet this higher power upon which we rely for the gift of life must itself be incapable of death, otherwise it, too, would be contingent upon another higher power, etc. This "higher power" upon which we rely is God.

---

13 See CCC 32–33.
14 To be contingent upon another is to be utterly dependent on it.

Second, consider the example that takes as its starting point the design of the universe. By observing the beauty and order of the world—not simply of what we experience here on earth, but even the amazing discoveries made about the design and order of the universe itself—we cannot help but consider that there must be an intelligent, creative designer who authored the world and all its beauty. Beauty cannot originate from chaos or mere happenstance; beauty is the expression of a supreme intelligence that has authored all things and sustains them with His power. God is indeed this ultimate designer.

In addition to these two examples of contingency and design, which provide evidence for God's existence from the perspective of the world around us, consider two additional examples that can be drawn by reflection upon the human person. First, since we are created to be with God as our supernatural end, no combination of purely natural ends can satisfy the deepest longings of the human heart. Sometimes a person may think that power, sex, fame, and wealth hold the key for being happy, but real and abiding happiness cannot be found in such finite and temporal things. Recall those famous words of St. Augustine we mentioned in chapter one, "Our hearts are restless, O Lord, until they rest in thee." The more we seek what the world offers us, the more restless we become, since nothing less than communion with the infinite God can truly satisfy us. Reflecting on St. Augustine's conversion, Pope Benedict XVI states:

> Even today, as in his time, humanity needs to know and
> above all to live this fundamental reality: God is love,
> and the encounter with him is the only response to the
> restlessness of the human heart; a heart inhabited by
> hope, still perhaps obscure and unconscious in many of
> our contemporaries but which already today opens us
> Christians to the future, so much so that St. Paul wrote
> that "in this hope we were saved" (Rom. 8:24).[15]

Another example of a proof of God's existence drawn from reflection on the human person focuses on the role of moral conscience, which

---

15 Pope Benedict XVI, General Audience of February 27, 2008.

calls us to seek the good and to avoid all evil. Whenever we freely commit a serious sin against God, we are plagued by pangs of guilt, which can actually be a positive experience. How can something as terrible as guilt be something positive? It brings to the level of our consciousness the fact that we broke communion with God, and that we must confess our sin and make atonement for it in order to be fully restored to friendship with God. No one enjoys feeling guilty, and if one were able to write the laws of an individual, subjective morality, one would make sure that nothing ever caused a feeling of guilt within us. The fact that we feel guilt after seriously sinning demonstrates that we are held responsible for breaking a law that we did not author. This objective law of right and wrong that we did not author, but to which we are held to obedience, is sufficient evidence for God's existence, since every law requires a lawgiver, and the only lawgiver of a timeless, trans-historical, trans-cultural moral law is God.

The fact that God's existence can be known through reason alone is instructive in helping us to understand better the issue of atheism, which the Second Vatican Council referred to as "one of the most serious problems of our time."[16] There are several reasons that may explain why a person becomes an atheist:[17] a response to evil and personal tragedy in the world; a decision not to be bound by a higher, objective moral code; and the poor example of theists themselves. What is central to each of these possible motives for becoming atheistic is that atheism is not an intellectual problem, but rather a moral and/ or psychological one. The problem is not that God did not give us sufficient evidence of His existence, but rather the problem is within the mental and/or psychological attitudes of the person who refuses to accept the evidence for God's existence. In some instances, the person may be fully responsible for his/her rejection of God, as is the case with a person who rejects God in order to become morally autonomous. In other situations, factors may be present that diminish the person's responsibility for rejecting God, such as a person who has just

---

16 Second Vatican Council, Pastoral Constitution on the Church in the Modern World *Gaudium et spes* (December 7, 1965), no. 19.

17 Generally speaking, an atheist is a person who rejects the existence of God, as distinct from an agnostic, who doubts whether we can really have sufficient knowledge as to whether God exists or not.

experienced a devastating tragedy in life due to the death of an innocent loved one.[18] Having recently experienced such a tragedy, I would like to suggest that tragic events are not only events that can potentially pull us away from God, but if we allow God to heal our emotions and memories, they can also be occasions for drawing us closer to God than we had ever been before. It does not happen overnight, and it cannot happen without both God's grace and our willingness. But if we trust in Him, He will never disappoint.[19] Atheism will forever remain a problem, and never a solution.

Faith and Reason

As we have seen, the use of reason is necessary before one can exercise the gift of faith,[20] and the evidence for God's existence that addresses itself to pure reason enables us to more readily accept the crowning of natural reason with the gift of supernatural faith. Reason tells us that God exists, yet faith is needed in order to enter into communion with Him. Reason points to the "fact" of God, yet faith is needed in order to access the "mystery" of God, and His plan for our salvation. Just as divine grace builds upon and perfects human nature rather than abolishing it or overruling it, so too does the theological virtue of faith build upon and perfect natural human reason.

In 1998, Pope John Paul II issued an encyclical[21] to the bishops of the Church addressing the relationship between faith and reason, which was aptly entitled *Fides et ratio* ("Faith and Reason"). The encyclical begins with these words, "Faith and reason are like two wings on which the human spirit rises to the contemplation of truth. . ." If we picture a dove trying to fly off a high branch with its left wing clipped, it will do no better than spiral downwards to its eventual destruction. And should the dove attempt to fly off the same branch with its right wing clipped instead of its left, the same outcome would be expected. In order for the dove to fly off the branch and maintain constant altitude, or even

---

18 See CCC 2125.

19 "And hope does not disappoint us, because God's love has been poured into our hearts through the Holy Spirit who has been given to us" (Romans 5:5).

20 Certainly the gift of faith can be *received* at any age; however, it cannot be *exercised* until one has the use of reason.

21 An encyclical is a formal teaching communicated by letter.

soar higher, both of its wings need to be working properly. Relating this analogy to the issue at hand, John Paul shows that to separate faith from reason results in either superstition (faith not grounded in reason) or futility in living for what is beneath the highest aspiration of the human heart (reason closed to the gift of faith). Faith and reason stand or fall together.[22]

Perhaps it is no coincidence that Pope John Paul II signed his encyclical *Fides et ratio* on September 14, which is the Feast of the Exaltation of the Holy Cross. Consider the following passage of St. Paul:

> Where is the wise man? Where is the scribe? Where is the debater of this age? Has not God made foolish the wisdom of the world? For since, in the wisdom of God, the world did not know God through wisdom, it pleased God through the folly of what we preach to save those who believe. For Jews demand signs and Greeks seek wisdom, but we preach Christ crucified, a stumbling block to Jews and folly to Gentiles, but to those who are called, both Jews and Greeks, Christ the power of God and the wisdom of God. (1 Cor. 1:20–24)

To the casual reader, a crucified messiah; a murdered God; a buried savior are all apparent contradictions, yet through the eyes of faith, these historical events bear a distinct eloquence as part of the divine plan. It is part of the mission of a Christian to educate non-believers, primarily through the example of one's own life, that they may be led from skepticism to truth; from ignorance to enlightenment; from hatred to love.

St. Peter exhorts us, "Always be prepared to make a defense to any one who calls you to account for the hope that is in you, yet do it with gentleness and reverence" (1 Pet. 3:15). The underlying fact of St. Peter's statement is that all the teachings of Christianity, every last one of them, are eminently reasonable, since one cannot be expected to make a defense, an *apologia*, for what is irrational. This point is crucial: although the mysteries of the Christian faith do indeed transcend

---

22 See Pope John Paul II, *Fides et ratio*, no. 48.

human reason by going beyond it,[23] and although they are inaccessible to pure human reason, they never contradict reason. It may not be immediately clear how there can be one God in three persons, but the doctrine of the Trinity does not violate reason. Similarly, we may not understand how God could become man and die, yet the truths of the Incarnation and Redemption do not defy reason. Never does the Church expect the believer to suspend reason in order to accept a teaching of the faith, but rather she summons her children to go beyond the limits of natural reason in embracing the supernatural truths of God's inner life and love.

Conclusion

We have briefly explored the mutual relationship between faith and reason, pointing out that they are both necessary in order for us to advance in the knowledge of truth. By cultivating the cardinal virtues, which are proper to human nature, and the theological virtues, which are proper to the life of grace, we are able with the help of God to advance in the life of holiness to which we are all called.[24]

---

23 Although God never contradicts reason, He does transcend it, and therefore one must be wary of attempts to "put God in a box," the misguided result of some good-intentioned philosophical currents of thought (especially within Scholasticism) that claim to be able to postulate *a priori* a comprehensive understanding of the metaphysical principles "binding" God and the applications of them to the realm of theology. If God truly is the Supreme Being (which He is), then it appears to be quite intellectually arrogant to dismiss these words of Scripture: "For my thoughts are not your thoughts, neither are your ways my ways, says the LORD. For as the heavens are higher than the earth, so are my ways higher than your ways and my thoughts than your thoughts" (Is. 55:8–9).

24 The cardinal virtues are prudence, justice, temperance and fortitude, and the theological virtues are faith, hope and charity. See also footnote 4 of this chapter.

Chapter 3

Introduction to Sacred Scripture

Overview

When we refer to the Sacred Scriptures, we are referring to the Bible. These terms, "Scripture" and the "Bible," are interchangeable with the distinction being in their roots, yet it is interesting that the Catechism only employs the term "Bible" four times, but employs the term "Scripture" nearly one hundred and twenty-five times.[1] "Scripture" comes from the Latin for "writing," whereas "Bible" comes from the Greek term that denotes a collection of "books." The Bible is divided into two main portions, the Old Testament and the New Testament. The Old Testament consists of forty-five or forty-six books (the number depends on whether Lamentations is included as part of the Book of Jeremiah, or whether it is left to itself), and spans from before creation until the time of the Maccabees, less than two centuries before Jesus. The New Testament consists of twenty-seven books, beginning with the four gospels and concluding with the Book of Revelation.

The Canon

The canon may be defined as the official list of divinely inspired books, all of which are contained in the Bible. It was the bishops of the Catholic

---

1 Frequency of word usage within the Catechism may be researched through the Vatican website, www.vatican.va

Church who, with the assistance of the Holy Spirit, recognized the canonical books from those that were non-canonical. The books of the Bible did not fall from the heavens and announce that they were truly from God, but rather they competed with many other works of antiquity for canonical recognition. It is important to realize that the bishops did not *confer* canonicity on an otherwise non-canonical book, but rather *recognized* the canonicity intrinsic to the book, due to the Holy Spirit's inspiration at the time of its authorship. A similar example can be drawn from the canonization of saints. When a pope canonizes a saint, he simply draws solemn attention to an already existing situation, namely, that the person is in heavenly glory. The pope does not put someone in heaven through the act of canonization, but rather draws our attention to the truth that the person is already in heaven, and therefore worthy of our emulation.

The canon can be distinguished further into protocanonical and deuterocanonical books. Protocanonical books are those biblical books of either the Old or New Testament that were indisputably accepted by the early Christians as divinely inspired. Most biblical books fall under this category. Deuterocanonical books, on the other hand, refer to those books of the Bible and portions of others that are regarded as inspired by Catholics and some others, but not without initial challenges being made against their canonicity in the early Church. There are seven deuterocanonical books of the Old Testament: Sirach, (also called Ecclesiasticus); the Wisdom of Solomon (also known simply as the Book of Wisdom); Tobit; Judith; Baruch; 1 Maccabees; and 2 Maccabees. Protestant denominations do not accept these books as canonical, and therefore they are missing from Protestant Bibles. We may also speak of deuterocanonical books of the New Testament, such as the Epistle to the Hebrews, the Book of Revelation, and the Epistle of James, to name just a few. Unlike the situation with the Old Testament, eventually all Christians did agree upon the acceptance of the deuterocanonical books of the New Testament, and to this day all Christians accept the same books of the New Testament.

It is noteworthy that the earliest authoritative list we possess of the canon of the entire Bible dates back to the end of the fourth century,[2] and

---

2   Decree of Pope Damasus in 382, as found in Denzinger, 84.

that list includes all the books found in the Catholic Bible today, including the deuterocanonical books that are missing from Protestant Bibles.

From what has been said thus far, it should be clear that one must not confuse the deuterocanonical books, which are divinely inspired and therefore canonical, with the apocryphal books. Apocryphal books are books that some people falsely claimed to have been inspired by God, and therefore, it is claimed, ought to have been included in the biblical canon. For example, whereas Catholics view a book like Wisdom of Solomon as deuterocanonical, Protestants view this book as apocryphal. In truth, however, the apocryphal books were not divinely inspired, and therefore did not belong in the biblical canon. Although apocryphal books cannot be entirely dismissed as having absolutely no truthful value (for example, we learn from them the names of Mary's parents, and the types of animals present at the birth of Jesus), they contain enough theological errors to seriously confuse anyone who does not already have a very solid grounding in the faith. They should not be read until the prospective reader has a strong foundation and understanding of the faith, otherwise the potential harm would far outweigh the potential good that could come from such reading.

Biblical Inspiration

In our daily lives, we sometimes find ourselves inspired by a variety of sources to go beyond the ordinary and to seek something greater. For those deeply involved in sports, this motivation may come through a professional athlete who excels in both the sport as well as in the moral life; for an artist, a picturesque sunset may be the source of inspiration for a magnificent poem, or a sublime painting. For a Christian, the saints are our "holy heroes," worthy of emulation, reminding us that ultimately Jesus Christ ought to be at the center of everything in our lives.

A common characteristic of these sources of inspiration is that they are external stimuli that encourage a positive, beyond-the-ordinary drive or zeal within us to accomplish a certain task. When we speak of "biblical inspiration," often we may think in terms similar to those already mentioned. In truth, however, the essence of biblical inspiration is more unlike and dissimilar from these previous examples than it is like them. The category of biblical inspiration is truly in a league of its own, and is worthy of further reflection.

The primary biblical foundation for the inspiration of the Bible is found in St. Paul's second letter to St. Timothy: "All Scripture is inspired by God and profitable for teaching, for reproof, for correction, and for training in righteousness, that the man of God may be complete, equipped for every good work" (2 Tim. 3:16–17). St. Paul directly intended these words to refer to the Old Testament, since at the time of his writing the New Testament was still in the process of being written. Yet the Church quickly understood that the full meaning of this passage equally applies to all of the canonical books, and not only to those of the Old Testament.

The term used by St. Paul to denote the Bible's divine inspiration is *theopneustos*, which may be translated as "God-breathed." To say that the Bible is "God-breathed" does not simply mean that the Bible is capable of motivating us to do something positive like poetic, aesthetic, or other forms of inspiration, but that it is imbued with the very breath of God to guide us towards our eternal salvation.

Since the Bible has received God's breath, it is worthwhile to consider the function of God's breath in salvation history. In the beginning of Genesis, chapter 2, God takes clay from the earth, and through His action of breathing into it, it becomes a living being. In the New Testament, Jesus breathes upon His disciples after His Resurrection from the dead, and they receive the Holy Spirit. In both of these instances, this breath, this divine kiss, signifies as well as actually bestows life and vitality. Adam, the first man, was given natural life, while Jesus' disciples become partakers in the supernatural life of God through the outpouring of the Holy Spirit.[3] For this reason it can be stated that "the word of God is living and active" (Greek: *energes*), i.e. energizing (Heb. 4:12).

The Second Vatican Council, restating the teaching passed down through Sacred Tradition, teaches that the whole Bible is inspired by God, and not merely parts of it.[4] This teaching means that there is no part of the Bible that can claim sole human authorship without concomitant divine authorship as well, no matter how apparently irrelevant the portion of Scripture being studied may seem (i.e. the

---

3 See John 20:22.
4 See CCC 105 and Second Vatican Council, *Dei Verbum*, no. 11.

clean and unclean laws of Leviticus, or the long names in the genealogy of Jesus as presented in Luke 3, etc.). It may be true that a prayerful reflection on the Parable of the Prodigal Son may powerfully motivate us to receive the much-needed Sacrament of Confession more so than reading the account of Abram tithing to Melchizedek in Genesis 14, yet both of these passages, as well as everything else in Scripture, are equally inspired by God.

THE PROCESS OF INSPIRATION

Just as the Bible is unlike any other book of human civilization, so also was the process of biblical inspiration an utterly unique phenomenon. The Holy Spirit supernaturally enlightened the minds of the authors of Scripture so that they set down in writing everything that He wanted, without error, with nothing added and nothing omitted, and when needed, divine Revelation would accompany biblical inspiration in order to teach the sacred authors truths that they might not have previously known.[5] On occasion it is maintained that God mechanically dictated word-for-word what was to be written down, yet this view is erroneous. The Church clearly refers to the "authors" of Scripture, yet if a person simply writes down what was dictated by another, then that writer remains a mere secretary, and not an author. Whereas a secretary writes down the insights of another, an author is the one who formulates the insights and is therefore the originator of the content. In the case of the Scriptures, God inspired the sacred authors in such a manner that everything God wanted written was written, but according to the common and individual mannerisms and abilities of the authors. The personalities of the human authors were not obscured, but enhanced through this divine collaboration. All of this is best summarized as follows: "In composing the sacred books, God chose men and while employed by Him they made use of their powers and abilities, so that with Him acting in them and through them, they, as true authors, consigned to writing everything and only those things which He wanted."[6]

---

5   Divine Revelation refers to the self-disclosure of God and His plan for our salvation. Divine Revelation, found in both Scripture and Tradition, came to an end with the death of St. John, the beloved apostle, about the year 96.

6   Second Vatican Council, *Dei Verbum*, no. 11.

As can be observed from what has been said, the way in which the Bible is inspired is utterly unique from any other form of inspiration. Even though God motivates us with His grace to live a life of holiness through written sources other than the Bible, such as the writings of the saints or prayers of the liturgy, the movement of the Holy Spirit illuminating the mind and heart of the faithful through these non-biblical works is quite distinct from His work of biblical inspiration. Theologically speaking, this charism[7] of biblical inspiration that was experienced (albeit unknowingly) by the biblical authors ended with the composition of the final books of the Bible and therefore has no counterpart in the contemporary Church. This point will be significant in the next chapter when we discuss biblical inerrancy.

Given that the doctrine of biblical inspiration pertains to a past charism that ended with the completion of the Scriptures and is therefore no longer active in the Church today, Christians may wonder if there is any role today for the Spirit to work within the hearts of the faithful. Indeed the same Spirit who inspired the sacred authors continues to work in the hearts of the faithful today. It is true that when Christians prayerfully read the Bible today, the Holy Spirit prompts them to be more dedicated and resolute in the Christian life. Yet this type of inspiration by the Spirit is different both in kind and degree from the Spirit's mode of operation in the apostolic and pre-apostolic period of the composition of the Scriptures, and may best be called "spiritual illumination" instead of "inspiration" to avoid confusing the two realities. Unlike the completed phenomenon of biblical inspiration, modern day spiritual illumination does not result in a supernatural elevation of the intellect, nor may it be accompanied by divine Revelation, nor is inerrancy guaranteed.[8]

---

7   "Charism" comes from the Greek term *charis* meaning "grace." The charism of biblical inspiration pertains to a free gift of the Holy Spirit given to selected, individual human persons in the past for the purpose of consigning the Word of God to a written form, that it could be known, preserved, and passed down to all generations.

8   It certainly is possible for any given project to be completed without formal error, just as it is possible for a student to score a 100 percent on any given exam. Although it is still *possible* for a purely human work to be without error, one cannot *guarantee* an inerrant outcome of a human undertaking without supernatural assistance.

Implications of Dual Authorship

God is at the origin of the Scriptures, and therefore He is the author of the Scriptures. Yet since the human collaborators were free to write the Bible according to their own ways of thinking and expression, they too are rightly called authors of the Scriptures. We call this dynamic interaction between the divine and human authors of Scripture the dual authorship of the Bible, and several points flow from this dynamic that must be respected if we are to interpret the Scriptures properly.

The Bible is the word of God *expressed in human language.* Since the Bible is authored by humans, it follows that in order to interpret it correctly we must take into consideration all those things that give us a better understanding of what the human authors intended to express, such as the historical time period in which the book was written; the person/ group/ audience to whom the book was addressed; the reasons the book was written; where the book was written and in which language; the command of language and literary genre(s) employed by the author; and the historical, cultural, political or religious state of affairs at the time, both with respect to the author and the target audience. The art of biblical criticism, using methods aimed at precision and objectivity, focuses on shedding light on these important questions.

The Bible is *the word of God* expressed in human language. The Bible is authored by God Himself, and the effective application of critical methods in studying the Bible is a necessary but insufficient means for properly interpreting the Scriptures. Even if we provide exhaustive answers to the questions raised by some of the aforementioned examples of biblical criticism, we still would have not yet arrived at a sufficient understanding of the Bible until we take into account the fact that the Bible requires the light of the Holy Spirit in order to interpret it correctly and effectively. After all, should we conclude that purely literary, historical and cultural approaches to biblical interpretation are sufficient to understand it, then we are really stating that the Bible is no greater than any other work of human literature. The reason the Bible is greater than any other work of literature in the history of civilization is because God Himself authored it, and living faith in Him is necessary to truly understand it.

Unfortunately, there are clearly two extremes on the exegetical landscape that need to be avoided. The first extreme is motivated by a rationalistic mentality, and it claims that there is nothing supernatural about the Bible itself, nor about the teachings it communicates. It is argued that miracles are impossible, and all such accounts of miracles in the Bible are embellishments in order to make it more appealing to its readers. This mindset further maintains that reason alone reigns supreme, and whatever cannot be demonstrated or proven through the senses does not exist. The second extreme is fideism, which is frequently found in fundamentalist circles. This extreme claims that all of the scientific methods used to interpret Scripture are irrelevant, and all that matters is having blind faith in God's word.

The truth of the matter is that since the Bible is truly the word of God in the words of men, we need both faith and reason, grace and nature, authentic trust in God and a solid intellectual grounding to interpret it properly.

Divine Condescension

It is beautiful to observe that God, who could have chosen to give us the Scriptures wholly on His own initiative without human cooperation, shows us through this divine-human collaboration of dual authorship how grace presupposes and elevates human nature rather than destroying it. How significant this reflection is for our daily lives as we understand that God works in us and through us, truly elevating our frail and lowly condition to become capable of participating in the very life of the Almighty! Such is the work of Divine condescension.

The term "condescension" often invokes negative and sometimes even painful images, such as a proud teacher making his students look foolish and feel insignificant, or a know-it-all making her friends feel ignorant and useless. These are indeed examples of condescension, but so also are the examples of a father who comes home to his nine-month-old girl, promptly snatching her up in his arms as he makes "goo-goo" and "da-da-da-da" sounds to her in order to communicate with her, and the example of a mother who answers her young children's questions about God in a different manner than the college students whom she will teach in class that evening.

"Condescension" simply means "coming down," and whereas negative expressions of condescension tend to make the recipient of these actions feel quite "low" due to the rude actions of another, positive expressions of condescension refer to a coming down to the level of another so that a mutual understanding may be reached. The inspiration of the Bible is a powerful example of divine condescension whereby the almighty and infinite God lowers Himself to our level by allowing His truth and message of salvation to be expressed in feeble, simple, limited human language.[9] In so doing, God reveals His great love for us, and desire that all of us spend eternity with Him. Yet even God's invitation to salvation as shown to us through the Bible is not the ultimate expression of divine condescension. The greatest example of God's condescension is the Incarnation itself, when God in becoming man came down to our level in order to elevate our entire being up to His. In chapter eight we will focus more upon the significance of the Incarnation.

Conclusion

The Bible has been entrusted to the Church as a powerful means through which we can grow in wisdom and knowledge concerning the truths of salvation. God entrusted to the Church His written word that was composed through the process of biblical inspiration. Neither God alone nor man alone was responsible for this undertaking, but rather the Bible is the fruit of the mutual collaboration between the divine and human authors. Because the Bible is expressed by humans in human language, it is necessary to study the human aspects of Scripture in order to understand it sufficiently, and because the Bible is also authored by almighty God, it is necessary to study the Scriptures with living faith. Only through the convergence of both faith and reason can we truly understand God's plan of salvation and His gift of eternal life that He offers to each one of us.

---

9   See CCC 101 and Second Vatican Council, *Dei Verbum*, no. 13.

Chapter 4

The Interpretation of Sacred Scripture

Overview

In this chapter we shall outline the basic principles for reading and interpreting the Bible according to God's purpose and meaning, as opposed to the commonplace practice of reading one's own private and sometimes erroneous meanings into the sacred text. To read the text in a way that seeks to "draw out" the meaning intended by God and the sacred authors is called *exegesis*, whereas to force our own meanings into the text is called *eisegesis*. We must always seek out God's message, even if such teachings make us uncomfortable by presenting a challenge to us to change our own lives. We are not to read Scripture in a haughty manner as if we were teaching God a lesson, but rather we are to read Scripture with a docile disposition so that God may teach us.[1]

Biblical Truthfulness

In the last chapter, we discussed the doctrine of biblical inspiration, which is directly related to the doctrine of the Bible's truthfulness. Pope Benedict XVI has observed, "Certainly theological reflection has always considered inspiration and truth as two key concepts for an

---

1   Citing the example of Pope Gregory the Great's methodology for interpreting Scripture, Pope Benedict XVI writes, "Intellectual humility is the primary rule for one who searches to penetrate the supernatural realities beginning from the sacred Book[s]" (General Audience of June 4, 2008).

ecclesial hermeneutic of the sacred Scriptures,"[2] and in a certain sense, these two doctrines stand or fall together.

The Catholic Church has always maintained that the Bible is inerrant, meaning that it is true in all of its affirmations and does not contain error. Consider the following teaching of the Second Vatican Council's Constitution on Divine Revelation, known also as *Dei Verbum*, expressed in the Catechism and Pope Benedict's Apostolic Exhortation *Verbum Domini:* "The inspired books teach the truth. 'Since therefore all that the inspired authors or sacred writers affirm should be regarded as affirmed by the Holy Spirit, we must acknowledge that the books of Scripture firmly, faithfully, and without error teach that truth which God, for the sake of our salvation, wished to see confided to the Sacred Scriptures.'"[3]

It is widely heard among Catholics that the doctrine of biblical inerrancy teaches that the Bible is without error in matters of faith and morals; however it might very well contain errors in other matters, especially history. This misunderstanding has a disastrous effect upon biblical interpretation because it invites interpreters to be "creative" in their understanding of history, allowing them to dispense with significant persons and events of salvation history. For example, some claim that Adam and Eve were purely mythical; while others argue that Moses was not a real person, but a symbolic representation of the collective wisdom of the people; and yet others deny that the event of the Exodus from Egypt ever took place. Examples of this type of thinking can be multiplied throughout the Old Testament and well into the New Testament.

The truth of the matter is that the entire Bible is inerrant, and that such inerrancy is not limited to matters of faith and morals only. It is crucial that the Church's teaching on this matter be understood, especially by the clergy, who hold considerable influence over the People of God through their preaching and catechesis. Once the inerrancy of the Bible is restricted (limited inerrancy), the value and usefulness of the entire Bible is called into question and the word of God quickly becomes muted and relegated to a lesser position of authority in the Christian life.

---

2   Pope Benedict XVI, *Verbum Domini*, no. 19.
3   CCC 107 and Pope Benedict XVI, *Verbum Domini*, no. 19.

We discussed biblical inspiration in the last chapter, and it was made clear that the *entire* Bible was inspired, and not only some or even most of it. Since the entire Bible is inspired, it follows that the entire Bible is authored by God Himself. If there were error in the Bible (for example, suppose that Moses never really existed, but was an imaginary figure who was invented in order to make the events of the Pentateuch seem more supernatural and dramatic), the author who stated the error (in our case, the author who clearly maintains the true historicity of Moses) would be responsible for that error. If part of the Pentateuch had been authored by God, and other parts of the Pentateuch authored only by man, one could argue that the human author(s) was/were in error, but God would not be responsible for it. Yet once we conclude that the entire Bible is inspired, it follows that there is no part of the Bible that could claim human authorship apart from divine authorship as well. In this case, the error would not only be committed by the human author(s), but by God Himself as the divine author. However, it is impossible for God, the perfect being, to err, or for Him to lead others into error. Therefore there can be no error in the Bible.

Consider also the fact that matters of faith and morals do not manifest themselves in a vacuum, but are gradually made known to us via divine Revelation through the medium of history in space and time. There is no "magic line" that indicates where matters of history end and matters of faith and morals begin. Consider, for example, the Resurrection of Jesus from the dead. Some will consider it primarily an event of faith, and therefore it must really have happened, since the Bible is at least trustworthy in matters of faith and morals. But the Resurrection is also a historical event that took place in time and space. If the Resurrection is viewed primarily as a historical event, and if the Bible is not inerrant in matters of history, then one could argue that the Resurrection never really happened. And there are some Christians who think this way, believing that they can invoke the authority of the Second Vatican Council to support their views. Perhaps now we are getting a glimpse at why the Catholic landscape is in such chaos and rebellion in many parts of the world, especially in America!

If a person is composing a work and has reason to believe that a certain passage may be grossly misunderstood according to what appears to be the plain sense of the passage, the author could modify the passage so that it would no longer be vague or confusing. The bishops of the Second Vatican Council surely would have realized that the relevant passage in *Dei Verbum*, no. 11 concerning inerrancy could be understood in conflicting ways, so they opted to insert a footnote to help clarify the proper meaning of the passage.[4] This footnote, which bears the same magisterial weight as the document itself, cites the following five authorities: St. Augustine; St. Thomas Aquinas; the Council of Trent; Pope Leo XIII; and Pope Pius XII. The significance of this footnote must not be underestimated; the actual citation for each of the above sources within the footnote indicates the very place where these sources each teach that it is impossible for any error to coexist with God's divine authorship, and that the inerrancy of the Bible is plenary (plenary inerrancy). As an example, consider the following excerpt from Pope Leo XIII's landmark encyclical on biblical studies, which is one of the five authorities cited in footnote #5 of *Dei Verbum*:

> So far is it from being possible that any error can co-exist with inspiration, that inspiration not only is essentially incompatible with error, but excludes and rejects it as absolutely and necessarily as it is impossible that God Himself, the supreme Truth, can utter that which is not true. This is the ancient and unchanging faith of the Church, solemnly defined in the Councils of Florence and of Trent, and finally confirmed and more expressly formulated by the Council of the Vatican. . . . It follows that those who maintain that an error is possible in any genuine passage of the sacred writings, either pervert the Catholic notion of inspiration, or make God the author of such error. And so emphatically were all the Fathers and Doctors agreed that the divine writings, as left by the hagiographers, are free from all error, that they laboured earnestly, with no less skill than reverence, to reconcile with each other those numerous passages which seem at variance—the very passages

---

4   The footnote reference to which we are alluding is no. 5.

which in great measure have been taken up by the "higher criticism;" for they were unanimous in laying it down, that those writings, in their entirety and in all their parts were equally from the *afflatus* of Almighty God, and that God, speaking by the sacred writers, could not set down anything but what was true.[5]

Additionally, Pope Pius XII considered the issue of inerrancy so important that he already addressed it in the opening paragraph of his encyclical on biblical studies (*Divino afflante spiritu*), which was written to commemorate the fiftieth anniversary of Pope Leo XIII's encyclical. This teaching of Pope Pius XII is also found cited in footnote number 5 of *Dei Verbum* 11:

> When, subsequently, some Catholic writers, in spite of this solemn definition of Catholic doctrine, by which such divine authority is claimed for the "entire books with all their parts" as to secure freedom from any error whatsoever, ventured to restrict the truth of Sacred Scripture solely to matters of faith and morals, and to regard other matters, whether in the domain of physical science or history, as "obiter dicta" and— as they contended—in no wise connected with faith, Our Predecessor of immortal memory, Leo XIII in the Encyclical Letter *Providentissimus Deus*, published on November 18 in the year 1893, justly and rightly condemned these errors and safe-guarded the studies of the Divine Books by most wise precepts and rules.[6]

Finally, consider the following words of St. Augustine, the greatest of the Latin Fathers of the Church, to St. Jerome, the greatest biblical commentator of the Fathers of the Church:

> On my part I confess to your charity that it is only to those Books of Scripture which are now called canonical that I have learned to pay such honour and

---

5 Pope Leo XIII, *Providentissimus Deus*, nos. 20–21, emphasis added.
6 Pope Pius XII, Encyclical Letter on Promoting Biblical Studies *Divino afflante spiritu* (September 30, 1943), no. 1.

reverence as to believe most firmly that none of their writers has fallen into any error. And if in these Books I meet anything which seems contrary to truth, I shall not hesitate to conclude either that the text is faulty, or that the translator has not expressed the meaning of the passage, or that I myself do not understand.[7]

In a spirit of true humility, exegetes[8] must understand that any error concerning biblical interpretation lies within us as fallible human persons, and not with God or with the Scriptures themselves. Perhaps this point is best expressed by St. Augustine, who wrote, "God wished difficulties to be scattered through the Sacred Books inspired by Him, in order that we might be urged to read and scrutinize them more intently, and, experiencing in a salutary manner our own limitations, we might be exercised in due submission of mind."[9]

Three Principles of Authentic Biblical Interpretation

Dei Verbum, the Second Vatican Council's Constitution on Divine Revelation, sets forth three vital principles for properly interpreting the Bible, which were formally incorporated into the Catechism.[10] These principles are all rooted in the realization that the same Holy Spirit who inspired the sacred authors to compose the sacred books of the Bible is also the same Spirit of truth who introduces us to the spiritual riches of the Bible as we devoutly read it or hear it proclaimed today.

The first principle for accurately interpreting the Bible is known as the canonical approach to biblical interpretation. This principle requires that we interpret the Bible as a unified whole, rather than as disassociated parts. Consider the following words of Pope Benedict XVI:

> The aim of this [canonical] exegesis is to read individual texts within the totality of the one Scripture, which then sheds new light on all the individual texts. Paragraph 12 of the Second Vatican Council's Constitution on

---

7   Cited by Pope Leo XIII in *Providentissimus Deus*, no. 21.
8   An exegete is a person engaged in exegesis, the drawing out of the meaning of the biblical text.
9   Cited by Pope Pius XII in *Divino afflante spiritu*, no. 45.
10 See CCC 112–114.

Divine Revelation had already clearly underscored this as a fundamental principle of theological exegesis: If you want to understand the Scripture in the spirit in which it is written, you have to attend to the content and to the unity of Scripture as a whole.[11]

To apply the canonical approach to interpretation, we need to be mindful of three things: the passage's remote context, its proximate context, and its immediate context.

The remote context of a passage refers to its relationship to other passages, literary units, or even whole books within the Bible that address the same issue or shed greater light upon it. For example, many people are familiar with God's test of Abraham, found in Genesis 22:1–14, where Abraham is commanded by God to sacrifice his only son, Isaac.[12] Yet many people are unaware of what Abraham was thinking as to why he would obey God's command and prepare to slay Isaac. This information is not made explicit until we encounter a mention of the matter in Hebrews 11:17–19, where it states,

> By faith Abraham, when he was tested, offered up Isaac, and he who had received the promises was ready to offer up his only son, of whom it was said, "Through Isaac shall your descendants be named." He considered that God was able to raise men even from the dead; hence he did receive him back and this was a symbol.

From this biblical text, we come to understand that Abraham's faith was so strong that he believed that he would not really be losing his son to the pangs of death if he sacrificed him according to God's command, but rather that God would resurrect Isaac from the dead and restore him. This more complete understanding of the biblical account of Genesis 22 is gained through an application of the canonical method of biblical interpretation.

---

11 Pope Benedict XVI, *Jesus of Nazareth* (New York: Doubleday, 2007), xviii.

12 Ishmael had been disinherited at this point, therefore Isaac really is reckoned as Abraham's only son, as stated in Genesis 22:2, "Take your son, *your only-begotten son* Isaac, whom you love . . ." (emphasis added).

In addition to the remote context of a passage, we must also be mindful of its proximate context, which includes the thematically connected verses and chapters that come directly before and after the account being studied. Although the aforementioned pericope[13] was Genesis 22:1–14, when we continue reading Genesis 22:15 and beyond, we learn that God again called to Abraham, but this time instead of testing him, He made a covenant with him on the basis of his faithfulness as demonstrated in his willingness to offer up his only son. Therefore an interpretation of the account narrated in Genesis 22:1–14 without reference or consideration given to Genesis 22:15–18 would be incomplete; indeed the Abrahamic covenant is a central theme of Genesis, and it is directly connected to the account of Abraham's great test found in the twenty-second chapter of Genesis.

Finally, in addition to the remote and proximate contexts of a passage, we must also pay careful attention to the immediate context of the passage. In the example of Abraham that we have been using, the immediate context spans Genesis 22:1–14, since these verses make up the substance of the account. Unlike the proximate and remote contexts that more clearly illuminate the full significance of a given pericope, identification of the immediate context is vital to gain a fundamental understanding of the specific matter at hand. To use an analogy of a birthday cake: The remote context of a passage can be compared to the candles, and the proximate context to the icing. Yet the immediate context is the cake itself. All three are needed for a clear understanding of the event—a birthday celebration—since a cake without icing may be a good treat, but it is not particularly indicative of a festive event; and a cake with icing but without candles would not bear the fullest meaning of this particular festive event as a birthday.

The second principle for a proper understanding of the Bible is interpreting the Bible within the living Tradition of the Church. Tradition is the sacred memory of the Church, enabling the Church to never lose sight of her foundation in Christ and her heavenly mission of being the new ark of salvation for the human race. Indeed, "Sacred Scripture is written principally in the Church's heart rather than in

---

13 A "pericope" (per REH keh pee) is a selection of text that can stand alone as a literary unit for analysis.

documents and records, for the Church carries in her Tradition the living memorial of God's Word, and it is the Holy Spirit who gives her the spiritual interpretation of the Scripture."[14] Within this rich and venerable Tradition, there is contained the voluminous spiritual insights of the great Fathers, Doctors, and saints of the Church that lie within the "heart of the Church," as we have discussed in Chapter One. Moreover, the sacred liturgy and Christian art also bear witness to the Sacred Tradition of the Church, and therefore they are normative for a proper understanding of the Scriptures. A commonly cited dictum, "*lex orandi, lex credendi*," reminds us that the law of prayer is the law of belief.

The third and final principle for a proper understanding of the Bible is to interpret the Bible with due attention to the analogy of faith. This principle means that the interpreter of the Bible must be guided by the doctrines already professed by the Church. St. Thomas Aquinas pointed out many centuries ago, that since both the light of reason and the light of faith come from the same God, it is impossible that the valid conclusions of human reason could contradict the tenets of a correctly professed faith. Leo XIII authoritatively expressed this same judgment: "For, seeing that the same God is the author both of the Sacred Books and of the doctrine committed to the Church, it is clearly impossible that any teaching can by legitimate means be extracted from the former, which shall in any respect be at variance with the latter."[15] If, for example, an exegete is convinced through scholarship that Jesus could not have intended to found the Church, then the exegete's academic conclusion is in contradiction with the Catholic profession of faith that Jesus intentionally and directly founded the Church. In this situation, the exegete would humbly have to accept the fact that his conclusion is wrong, rather than argue that the Church or even God Himself is wrong in a theological matter that so closely touches upon the truths of our faith. In this way, the doctrines of the Church function as lights that illuminate and demarcate the walking path. Just as we would not want to stumble in the dark and fall to our death off a cliff because we ignored the illumination that comes from a flashlight,

---

14 CCC 113.
15 Pope Leo XIII, *Providentissimus Deus*, no. 14.

neither do we want to ignore the spiritual lights God has given to us along the path of salvation, beyond which lies the snares of doubt, skepticism, and pride of the Evil One.

The Senses of Scripture

The phrase "senses of Scripture" pertains to the meanings that Scriptural passages relay to us. When we use the term "sense," we are intending it as a way of illustrating the depth of meaning of a particular biblical passage. As the Catechism reminds us, there are two main senses of Scripture, the literal and the spiritual. The spiritual sense is then subdivided into three sections: the allegorical, the moral, and the anagogical.[16]

The literal sense is the starting point and foundation for the other senses, and without a proper understanding of the literal sense, one will not be able to properly discern and understand the spiritual sense of Scripture. When we speak of the literal sense of Scripture, we refer to the meaning of the given passage(s) as intended by the sacred author, and not simply the apparent meaning of the written word based on our understanding of what words should or could mean. In order to accurately discern the intention of the sacred author, consideration of literary form(s) is essential, as highlighted by the Second Vatican Council:

> To search out the intention of the sacred writers, attention should be given, among other things, to "literary forms." For truth is set forth and expressed differently in texts which are variously historical, prophetic, poetic, or of other forms of discourse. The interpreter must investigate what meaning the sacred writer intended to express and actually expressed in particular circumstances by using contemporary literary forms in accordance with the situation of his own time and culture. For the correct understanding of

---

16 Consider the remarks of Pope Benedict XVI on the senses of Scripture: "There are dimensions of the word that the old doctrine of the fourfold sense of Scripture pinpointed with remarkable accuracy. The four senses of Scripture are not individual meanings arrayed side by side, but dimensions of the one word that reaches beyond the moment" (*Jesus of Nazareth*, xx).

> what the sacred author wanted to assert, due attention must be paid to the customary and characteristic styles of feeling, speaking and narrating which prevailed at the time of the sacred writer, and to the patterns men normally employed at that period in their everyday dealings with one another.[17]

For example, Psalm 113:3 states, "From the rising of the sun to its setting the name of the Lord is to be praised!" The obvious meaning of this passage as intended by the author is to affirm that God's name ought to be extolled at all times. Note, however, that the passage is not intended to affirm that the sun actually moves upwards in the morning by physically "rising," and then descends again at night when it physically "sets."[18] As can be seen, when we speak of the literal sense of Scripture, we are contrasting it with a Fundamentalist understanding that would divorce the biblical statement from the intentionality of the sacred author.

Another example to better understand the literal sense of a passage can be drawn from the first chapter of Genesis. A Fundamentalist interpretation would allege that the earth was actually created in six twenty-four hour days because the passage mentions creation in six days. The problem with this interpretation, however, is that it does not consider how the sacred author is employing the term "day," which in Hebrew (*yom*) admits of several different meanings, ranging from a twenty-four hour span of time to an indefinite period of time.

Let's look to another example from the Gospels: a Fundamentalist reading of the passages concerning the "brothers of the Lord" in the Gospels leads a significant number of interpreters erroneously to conclude that these brothers must have been biological, full blood-brothers of Jesus, not recognizing (or ignoring) the fact that the Greek term employed for "brothers" (*adelphoi*) also has a variety of possible meanings, ranging from true blood-brothers to kinsmen. More will be said about this particular example in a later chapter.

---

17 Second Vatican Council, *Dei Verbum*, no. 12.
18 We know that the earth's rotation about its axis contributes to when it gets light and when it gets dark, and not any actual movement of the sun "rising" or "setting," yet such an accommodated form of speaking is universally accepted even today as it was in biblical times.

Allow me to share an exercise I did with my students in order to better illustrate the importance of a proper understanding of the senses of Scripture. I wrote the term "Die" on the blackboard and asked my students what concept I was communicating through that word, and the students promptly responded that I was referring to the concept of death. To their amazement, I told them that they were all wrong, because my intention was not to communicate the thought of death, but rather my intention was to talk with them about "Die Frau," meaning "the woman" in the German language. I proceeded to write the same term "Die" on the board a second time, and again I asked the students what I meant by that term. Again, they replied (although hesitantly this time) with the concept of death. Wrong again, I told them! My intention that time was to follow it with the term "septimo" in order to discuss the meaning of the biblical phrase, "the seventh day." Finally, a third time I wrote the term "Die" on the board and asked my students what I meant by that term. One student from the back immediately blurted out, "We have no idea!"

As shown through this simple exercise, we have no certain idea what is being communicated to us through the Bible if we do not take into account the intention of the sacred author. The reason why we must discern the meaning intended by the sacred author is due to the fact that God did not simply dictate what was to be written as a professional does to his secretary, but rather God empowered the human authors to communicate what He wanted revealed in the way that they thought would best accomplish this purpose, as we explained in the last chapter when discussing the doctrine of biblical inspiration. Since the sacred authors truly contributed to this divine project, it is imperative to discern what they meant by the words and phrases that they used. Then will we be able to discover what God intended to be communicated through their words, and only then can we rightly invoke the doctrine of biblical inerrancy to guarantee the truth of the content expressed by the sacred authors.

In addition to the literal sense, the second general sense of Scripture is the spiritual sense, which admits of three levels. Since the sacred authors are necessarily attempting to communicate a knowable content through their use of words, every passage has a literal sense; however it is not necessary for every passage to have a spiritual sense. The three-fold spiritual sense can be defined as that meaning intended by God, but not intended by the human author. As an example, consider the selection from Genesis 22:1–14 that we referred to earlier involving Abraham and Isaac. The literal sense of that account is fairly straight forward, given its genre of historical narrative. Yet that pericope is replete with the allegorical sense of Scripture (which we will come to shortly). Did the author of Genesis realize the allegorical significance of this pericope? No, since the only way he could have would have been if God gave to him a direct revelation of such, and if such a direct revelation were given, it seems reasonable to assume that such a fact would have been mentioned in the account, or even later in Genesis. Thus the senses of Scripture operate at two levels: the meaning known and intended by the sacred author (the literal sense), and the meaning intended by God, but not the sacred author (the spiritual sense).

There are three spiritual senses. The first spiritual sense is the allegorical sense, whereby the passage finds its ultimate fulfillment in the context of Christ and the Church. To identify just a few examples of Old Testament events with clear and sustained allegorical fulfillments, consider the crossing of the Red Sea fulfilled in Christian baptism; the Passover fulfilled in the Last Supper and Jesus' death on the Cross; the roles of the twelve tribes of Israel fulfilled in the twelve apostles; and the manna and quail given to the Israelites in the wilderness fulfilled in the Eucharist.[19] An even more extended allegorical fulfillment is found in typology, whereby a "type" usually found in the Old Testament is a prefigurement of its "antitype" in the New Testament. Returning again to Genesis 22:1–14, consider the following typological relationships: Isaac is the only beloved son of his father, Abraham, just as Jesus is the only beloved son of his Father; Isaac is to be sacrificed in the land of Moriah, just as Calvary is part of the mountain range known as Moriah; wood is essential for Isaac's sacrifice, just as the wood of the Cross is essential for Jesus' sacrifice; Isaac cries out, "My Father" and Jesus cries

---

19 The Eucharist is the sacrament of the Real Presence of the Body, Blood, Soul and Divinity of Jesus Christ under the appearances of bread and wine. It is the central sacrament of the Catholic Church. Unlike most non-Catholic Christians who believe that the Eucharist is merely a symbol of Jesus, Catholics firmly maintain that the Eucharist *is* Jesus Christ, as clearly taught in the sixth chapter of John's Gospel.

out, "My God, My God;" Isaac was a willing victim who did not fight his father to survive, just as Jesus was obedient to his Father in all things, even death; Abraham is told that God would provide the lamb for the sacrifice, just as Jesus is shown to be the Lamb of God, the lamb of sacrifice in the New Testament. There are numerous other parallels between this account in Genesis and the sacrifice of Jesus Christ in the New Testament. These typological relations are not coincidental, but intended by God as the allegorical sense of Scripture.

A second spiritual sense is the moral sense, whereby the biblical passage instructs us how properly to act in the light of Christ. Throughout the Bible, we are reminded of our own sinfulness and inadequacy so that we place our trust in God and invite His grace into our lives. As St. Augustine reminds us, "the law was given so that grace might be sought, and grace was given so that the law might be fulfilled." It is through divine grace that we become capable of persevering in holiness by keeping the flame of divine charity burning strongly within our soul and keeping the moral law, thereby living already in this life the way the saints live for all eternity in heaven.

The final spiritual sense is known as the anagogical[20] sense, which denotes how biblical passages remind us of our summons to eternal life. We recall that God desires the salvation of all persons without exception[21] and thus the invitation to eternal life is not given only to a select few, but it is offered to all. Passages exemplifying the anagogical sense enkindle the hope in our hearts not only for our own salvation, but also for the salvation of everyone.

Conclusion

Although reason alone cannot prove the fact that the Bible is divinely inspired, if one accepts by faith the fact that the Bible is inspired, then it necessarily follows through reason that the Bible must also be inerrant. Although many persons claim that Vatican II changed the Church's teaching on biblical inerrancy, the Council did no such thing, but rather reaffirmed the traditional teaching. By understanding and respecting the three principles of biblical interpretation coupled

---

20 From Greek *anagoge*, meaning "leading upwards."
21 See 1 Timothy 2:3–4.

with the senses of Scripture as explained in this chapter, the student of Scripture will be safeguarded against many of the errors in biblical interpretation that lead to falsehoods about God and His teachings. Fidelity to these principles, coupled with docility to the promptings of the Holy Spirit, will truly render biblical study both academically productive and spiritually enriching.

Chapter 5

Divine Revelation

Overview

Divine Revelation, also known as Public Revelation or simply "Revelation" (with a capital "R"), refers to the self-disclosure of God and His plan for our salvation. We may speak of three ways by which God's Revelation is made accessible to us: Sacred Scripture, Sacred Tradition, and the Magisterium. Although they do not all have the same importance, each of these components is essential in order for us to fully appreciate the beautiful deposit of faith that God has entrusted to His Church.

It is important not to confuse divine Revelation with what we call "private revelation." Instances of private revelation frequently include visions of Jesus or Mary experienced by certain individuals throughout history. Perhaps the most famous examples of private revelation are the apparitions of Mary in Fatima, Portugal[1] and Lourdes, France.[2] Whereas we discover through divine Revelation truth about God and His plan for our salvation, which we never knew before, no "new truth"

---

1 Our Lady of Fatima's feast day is May 13, commemorating her appearances to three children, Francisco, Jacinta, and Lucia in 1917.
2 The feast day of Our Lady of Lourdes is on February 11, commemorating her appearances to St. Bernadette Soubirous. Significantly, it was also on this feast day in 1984 that Pope John Paul II issued his Apostolic Letter on Human Suffering *Salvifici doloris*, and on this feast day in 2013 Pope Benedict XVI officially announced his resignation from the Petrine Office.

could ever come from an authentic instance of private revelation. The purpose of private revelation is to remind the members of the Church of elements already contained in divine Revelation that may have become ignored or at least not taken seriously. Whereas divine Revelation is like the seed, private revelation is like the sun and rain that waters the seed and gives it nourishment so that it can fully take root in the minds and hearts of contemporary Christians.[3]

Scripture

We have already defined Scripture as the inspired and inerrant word of God, through which God discloses to us the mystery of His innermost life, as well as His plan for our salvation. Scripture is part of the deposit of Revelation, meaning that we find in Scripture truths that we otherwise could not know about God, truths that are foundational to Christian faith and life.[4] Taken together with Sacred Tradition, Sacred Scripture is part of the Church's deposit of faith. The Scriptures are therefore clearly authoritative in the life of the Church, as St. Jerome alluded to in his famous statement, "Ignorance of Scripture is ignorance of Christ."

While it is true that the New Testament is the focus of Christianity, we must never forget the perennial value of the Old Testament. Often Christians ask, "Why should we study the Old Testament? Don't Christians only need to read the New Testament, particularly the Gospels?" Only through a solid understanding of the history, theology, rituals, and culture of the Old Testament period can we fully appreciate the mystery of Jesus, who lived as a Jewish male in the region of Palestine, embracing the normal and common cultural and religious practices of the late Old Testament period.

---

3   "A private revelation can introduce new emphases, give rise to new forms of piety, or deepen older ones. It can have a certain prophetic character (cf. 1 Thess. 5:19–21) and can be a valuable aid for better understanding and living the Gospel at a certain time; consequently it should not be treated lightly. It is a help which is proffered, but its use is not obligatory" (Pope Benedict XVI, *Verbum Domini*, 14).

4   This is not to deny that we also find within the Sacred Scriptures truths which we could, in fact, know through reason apart from Revelation, such as the precepts of the Ten Commandments. Yet it is fitting that such things are still communicated to us by God, so that we can all have absolute certainty about them without error or confusion.

Since the New Testament presupposes, builds upon and perfects the Old Testament, much of the New Testament would not make sense to us if we neglected the Old Testament. Perhaps St. Augustine said it best when relating the New and Old Testaments, "The New is hidden in the Old, and the Old is unveiled in the New." Consider also the following excerpt, "The unity of the two Testaments proceeds from the unity of God's plan and his Revelation. The Old Testament prepares for the New and the New Testament fulfills the Old; the two shed light on each other; both are true Word of God" (CCC 140). Indeed Sacred Scripture—both Old and New Testaments—is vital for us to understand God's Revelation to us, for which reason we devoted prior chapters to biblical matters.

Tradition

With Scripture, Sacred Tradition also constitutes the deposit of faith. As the Second Vatican Council has clarified, it is not the case that there are two deposits of faith, but rather both Scripture and Sacred Tradition together comprise one single deposit of faith. Sacred Tradition may be understood as the living memory of the Church, by which she passes down to every generation all that she is, and all that she believes.[5] Whereas many key teachings of the Church are found directly in Scripture, there are other teachings that are found or fully developed only through Sacred Tradition. The Second Vatican Council taught:

> Hence there exists a close connection and communication between sacred tradition and Sacred Scripture. For both of them, flowing from the same divine wellspring, in a certain way merge into a unity and tend toward the same end. For Sacred Scripture is the word of God inasmuch as it is consigned to writing under the inspiration of the divine Spirit, while sacred tradition takes the word of God entrusted by Christ the Lord and the Holy Spirit to the Apostles, and hands it on to their successors in its full purity, so that led by the light of the Spirit of truth, they may in proclaiming it preserve this word of God faithfully, explain it, and make it more widely known.[6]

5   See CCC 78.
6   CCC 82 and Second Vatican Council, *Dei Verbum*, no. 9.

The attentive reader may be puzzled with the above statements, thinking of St. Paul's instruction found in Colossians 2:8, "See to it that no one makes a prey of you by philosophy and empty deceit, according to human tradition, according to the elemental spirits of the universe, and not according to Christ." Indeed many Protestant Christians utterly reject the Catholic Church's claim of an authoritative Sacred Tradition based upon their mistaken interpretation of these words of St. Paul. We must clarify that St. Paul is speaking merely of human tradition, those practices developed and modified by men, whereas the Sacred Tradition of the Catholic Church is not human in origin, but ultimately from God and based on the teaching of Christ handed down through the apostles and their successors. Let us take a moment to probe this important difference between "divine" and "human" tradition.

Consider the example of celebrating the Thanksgiving holiday here in the United States. The majority of Americans celebrate Thanksgiving with a main dish of turkey, and if we were to ask any given family why they celebrate with turkey instead of, say, roast beef sandwiches, the family would more than likely reply that it is a "tradition" to eat turkey on Thanksgiving. What constitutes such a tradition? The fact that the practice of eating turkey on Thanksgiving was passed down from parents to their children for many generations. Yet is it absolutely necessary that one eat turkey on Thanksgiving as a way of celebrating this holiday? No, it is not. In fact, a number of people choose not to eat turkey for a variety of reasons, including a dislike of turkey, allergies, or a preference for a vegetarian diet. The principle at work here is that the eating of turkey on Thanksgiving is a tradition, a specifically human tradition, and since the tradition is human in origin, it can readily be changed by humans without issue. Certainly no one who refuses to eat turkey on Thanksgiving may be considered anti-American because of it!

In contrast to the above, let us consider the issue of a male-only priesthood. In our 21st century, there are a significant number of persons, both Catholic and non-Catholic, who argue that women should be admitted to the priesthood. The central argument goes something like this: Jesus called all people to Himself as disciples, both women and men, and although Jesus did not call women to be His apostles due to the social taboos of His time, there is no compelling reason why women should not be allowed to become priests in our current society other than the efforts of a male-dominated Church to preserve their own power. Such an argument misses the point completely. Jesus chose only men to be His apostles not because of some social taboo (Jesus certainly did not conform to popular opinions in either His moral or doctrinal teaching, as the Gospels make clear!), but because in God's design it is essential for a priest to be male (after all, being male is part of the man's being, and not simply a superficial attribute of the person). There is not any clear prohibition in the Bible against women becoming priests; however, within the memory of the Church through Sacred Tradition, it is abundantly clear that the reservation of the priesthood to men alone is a teaching rooted in Jesus Christ Himself, passed down since apostolic times through Sacred Tradition, and since this Tradition does not have its origin in any human person, but comes from God Himself, it is unable to be changed, even by the pope.[7] It is not a question of equal rights (since no one has the right to the priesthood; it is a gift), nor is it a question of women being second-class citizens (consider the example of the Virgin Mary who is exalted above all the other angels and saints); it is simply God's decision to which the Church herself is bound and powerless to change.[8]

While it is true that many of the teachings of our faith are found directly in Scripture, there are also teachings of our faith that are not clearly found in Scripture, but are found in Sacred Tradition, as evidenced through the above example. The Second Vatican Council stated, "Consequently it is not from Sacred Scripture alone that the Church draws her certainty about everything which has been revealed. Therefore both sacred tradition and Sacred Scripture are to be accepted and venerated with the same sense of loyalty and reverence."[9] Both Sacred Scripture and Sacred Tradition come from God Himself, and consequently they are both equally authoritative. Unlike Protestant Christianity, which rejects Sacred Tradition and elevates the Bible to the status of the supreme rule of faith,[10] Catholicism maintains that both

---

7   This issue is taken up again later in this chapter.
8   See CCC 1577–1578.
9   Second Vatican Council, *Dei Verbum*, no. 9.
10 Consider the motto of the Protestant Reformation, "sola Scriptura!" meaning, "the Bible alone!" as the sole rule of faith.

Sacred Scripture and Sacred Tradition together constitute the rule of faith. The Catholic position not only reflects the actual two-thousand-year-old practice of the Church from its founding through today, but it also is exceedingly reasonable. If we probe this issue a bit more, one can rightly ask why the *mode* of communication should matter. For example, if I wish to express my love for my wife, it would make little difference whether I expressed it through a letter, an email, or in the context of a telephone conversation. The mode of communication—whether by written letter, electronic email, or spoken conversation—matters little. The significance is not determined by the *mode* of communication, but by its *content*, the message. Similarly, the early Christians did not care whether the teachings of Christ were passed down to them in writing (the Bible) as distinct from oral transmission (Sacred Tradition). What was of crucial significance was the content.

At the time of the 16th century, the Protestant reformers distilled their beliefs into one phrase: *sola Scriptura*! For them, the Bible alone is the sole rule of faith and any claim to an authoritative Sacred Tradition was rejected. The Catholic response known as the Counter-Reformation espoused a theological principle of its own: *sola verbum Dei*! This Catholic position acknowledges that the Bible is indeed the Word of God, and therefore authoritative for faith and life. However, it also clarifies that the Bible is not the *only* place where we find the true Word of God. This second channel whereby we receive the Word of God is Sacred Tradition. Whereas Protestantism clings to the Bible alone, Catholics cling to the Word of God as found in both the Bible and Sacred Tradition. As has been stated, the crucial fact is that God gave to us His teaching for our salvation, and God entrusted all such Revelation to both Scripture and Tradition.

The practical and theological problems with the Protestant *sola Scriptura* position are significant. First, consider the fact that all Christians accept the same twenty-seven books of the New Testament; this fact includes Protestants who advocate the *sola Scriptura* principle. But there is no place in the Bible where we are given through divine inspiration an official list of the inspired books, and while it is true that there is a good amount of cross-referencing found in the New Testament, it is also true that even pagan literature is quoted,[11] so mere

---

11 See 1 Corinthians 15:33.

cross-referencing is an insufficient guarantor of canonicity. As was mentioned in a previous chapter, the biblical canon was authoritatively announced towards the close of the fourth century as the fruit of deliberations among the Catholic bishops of the early Church. The task was a difficult one precisely because there was no divinely generated list to follow, so the bishops prayed to the Holy Spirit to enlighten them as they made their decisions. The entire process is a work of Sacred Tradition, and to this day all Christians (perhaps unconsciously) reveal their belief in an authoritative Sacred Tradition every time they open the written Word of God. Thus the actual practice of Christianity refutes the *sola Scriptura* principle.

Second, consider that the Protestant axiom of "the Bible alone" means that everything needed for belief is contained within the Bible. According to this belief, if something is not clearly stated in the Bible, then it is not necessary for faith. Yet in no place does the Bible ever teach that it is the sole rule of faith. Protestants, therefore, are using a non-biblical principle in order to argue for the necessity of the Bible alone being our teacher in all matters of faith and morals. Again we have an example of a firm belief of historical Protestantism that violates the very principle that it claims to uphold.

Third, not only is *sola Scriptura* an unbiblical principle, as was shown above, but it is also an anti-biblical principle. The Bible clearly contains teachings that validate the importance of Sacred Tradition, thereby refuting a *sola Scriptura* principle. Consider 2 Thessalonians 2:15, which states, "So then, brethren, stand firm and hold to the traditions which you were taught by us, either by word of mouth or by letter." St. Paul is telling his fellow Christians to stand firm and maintain the traditions taught by us, i.e. the apostles, whether those traditions were manifested through word of mouth (Sacred Tradition) or through letter (Sacred Scripture). The primary books of the New Testament canon that are direct products of oral proclamation are the Gospels.[12] The Gospels are directly based on the life and teachings of Jesus Himself, passed down orally by those who encountered Jesus, highlighting the things that He really did and said. After receiving the gift of the Holy Spirit, the evangelists finally wrote down the four

---

12 See CCC 126.

Gospels. As can be seen through this sequence, Sacred Tradition came before the written word, with nothing becoming part of the written word that was not already part of the Sacred Tradition that preceded it. To reject the authority of Sacred Tradition, then, would effectively impair the authority and reliability of the written Gospels, which are the most central documents of the entire Bible.

Other passages that further reveal the anti-biblical nature of the *sola Scriptura* principle can be found in the Gospel of John. John 20:30 states, "Now Jesus did many other signs in the presence of the disciples, which are not written in this book" and John 21:25 states, "But there are also many other things which Jesus did; were every one of them to be written, I suppose that the world itself could not contain the books that would be written." It is abundantly clear that the early Church had no limited understanding of divine Revelation that included only the written word of God and not the preached word. It is a significant fact that although Jesus commanded His disciples to preach, he never once commanded them to write. The mode of communication (whether in writing or passed down orally) matters little; what is essential is the content communicated, not the mode by which the content is communicated.

The literary genius J.R.R. Tolkien authored the widely popular *Lord of the Rings* series as literary fiction that spans approximately thirteen months of narrative time from the beginning to the end of Frodo's journey. The three books comprising this trilogy total in excess of one thousand pages. Now compare this with the four Gospels, which give the accounts not of a fictitious hero's adventures, but of the real teachings and deeds of the Son of God who came to bring Redemption to the whole world. If we add up the pages of the Gospels, we arrive at only a small fraction of the number of pages found in the *Lord of the Rings* trilogy, with much of it consisting of repetitive information common to the three synoptic Gospels. Are we to conclude that three years of ministry of God-become-man is less exciting and noteworthy than thirteen months of a work of literary fiction? Of course not! The early Christians never suspected the Gospels of being exhaustive accounts. The evangelists selected only those elements of Jesus' ministry that were directly relevant to their individual audiences and purposes, and never claimed to give a comprehensive account of everything Jesus said or did for His three last years.

The Magisterium

The Magisterium refers to the official teaching body of the Church, consisting of the pope and bishops in union with him. Unlike both Sacred Scripture and Sacred Tradition, the Magisterium does not constitute part of the deposit of faith. Whereas we discover previously unknown truths about God and His plan for our salvation in both Sacred Scripture and Sacred Tradition, no such discovery can be made through the Church's Magisterium. For this reason the Second Vatican Council clearly states, "This teaching office is not above the word of God, but serves it, teaching only what has been handed on, listening to it devoutly, guarding it scrupulously and explaining it faithfully in accord with a divine commission and with the help of the Holy Spirit, it draws from this one deposit of faith everything which it presents for belief as divinely revealed."[13] Some distinctions are in order here: according to *what they are*, Sacred Scripture and Sacred Tradition, which are equally important, are superior to the Church's Magisterium. However, according to *what they do*, Sacred Scripture, Sacred Tradition, and the Magisterium are all essentially equal.

Consider the example of a treasure chest that contains precious valuables, partly consisting of pearls, and partly consisting of gold coins. The treasure represents divine Revelation, and the two forms of precious treasure represent Sacred Scripture and Sacred Tradition. You are the intended recipient of the treasure; however, when you approach the treasure chest to take possession of it, you notice that it is locked. As valuable as the contents of the treasure chest may be, the contents are not useful to you if you cannot access them. It is the Magisterium, however, which offers you the key, and with the Magisterium's help, you are now able to gain access to the treasure. The Magisterium did not add anything to the treasure that was not already there, but its function was to make accessible the treasure, to distribute the treasure to you as its beneficiary, and also to protect the treasure from efforts by others to replace it with counterfeit items.

As can be seen, according to their respective functions, Sacred Scripture, Sacred Tradition and the Magisterium are like the three legs of a tripod. If even one of the three legs of the tripod is removed—and

---

13 Second Vatican Council, *Dei Verbum,* no. 10.

it matters not which one—then the whole thing will come crashing down. As stated by the Second Vatican Council: "It is clear therefore, that in the supremely wise arrangement of God, Sacred Tradition, Sacred Scripture, and the Magisterium of the Church are so connected and associated that one of them cannot stand without the others. Working together, each in its own way, under the action of the one Holy Spirit, they all contribute effectively to the salvation of souls."[14]

The Pope

St. Jerome, one of the greatest interpreters of Sacred Scripture, once wrote concerning his obedience to the pope, "I am with whoever is united to the teaching of St. Peter."[15] And these words were not easy for St. Jerome to put into action, since he had a very strong temperament and did not always personally agree with the pope in matters of controversy.[16] Yet in the end, he always rendered obedience to the pope. The pope is the Vicar of Christ on earth, meaning that the pope is the visible representative and head of the Church on earth who speaks authoritatively in the name of Jesus Christ. Concerning the scope of the pope's authority, the Second Vatican Council observes, "For the Roman Pontiff, by reason of his office as Vicar of Christ, and as pastor of the entire Church has full, supreme, and universal power over the whole Church, a power which he can always exercise unhindered."[17]

As we have already seen, it is noteworthy that the Council explicitly teaches that the Magisterium "is not above the word of God, but serves it. . ."[18] Many people mistakenly think that the pope can teach whatever he wants about faith and morals, but this is not the case. Even the pope is bound to the teachings that originate from Jesus Christ, and not even the pope has the authority to change such things. The pope is indeed the "servant of the servants of God."

14 Ibid., no. 10 and CCC 95.
15 St. Jerome, as cited by Pope Benedict XVI, General Audience of November 14, 2007.
16 For example, St. Jerome did not favor the inclusion of the deuterocanonical books of the Old Testament into the Bible, contrary to his contemporary St. Augustine. But when the pope agreed with Augustine's assessment and ordered that the disputed books be included in the Vulgate, Jerome consented.
17 CCC 882 and Second Vatican Council, The Dogmatic Constitution on the Church *Lumen gentium* (November 21, 1964), no. 22.
18 Second Vatican Council, *Dei Verbum*, no. 10.

Jerusalem is the cradle of Christianity, since there Jesus suffered, died, rose again from the dead, and ascended into heaven. It is where the first Mass was celebrated and where the powerful outpouring of the Holy Spirit took place on Pentecost, the birthday of the Church. Yet with the event of the martyrdom of St. Peter on the Vatican hill, the center of Christianity was moved from Jerusalem to Rome. From the time of Peter through our present pope, there has always been a constant succession of popes who have their foundation in Jesus Christ. Through this unbroken chain of apostolic succession, the Catholic Church reveals itself as the only Christian church that has a historically verifiable, visible link extending back to Jesus Christ Himself who granted to Peter the authority and office that later became called the papacy. The biblical foundation for the papacy can be found in the following passage from Matthew's Gospel:

> Now when Jesus came into the district of Caesarea Philippi, he asked his disciples, "Who do men say that the Son of man is?" And they said, "Some say John the Baptist, others say Elijah, and others Jeremiah or one of the prophets." He said to them, "But who do you say that I am?" Simon Peter replied, "You are the Christ, the Son of the living God." And Jesus answered him, "Blessed are you, Simon Barjona! For flesh and blood has not revealed this to you, but my Father who is in heaven. And I tell you, you are Peter, and on this rock I will build my Church, and the gates of Hades shall not prevail against it. I will give you the keys of the kingdom of heaven, and whatever you bind on earth shall be bound in heaven, and whatever you loose on earth shall be loosed in heaven." (16:13–19)

Examining this passage, we can make several observations directly relevant to the institution of the papacy. First, Simon's name is changed to "Peter," meaning "rock." Divinely instituted name changes are rare in the Bible, and when they do occur, they signify a change in mission. Second, this new mission entrusted to Peter is to be the head of the Church after Jesus returns to heavenly glory after His Resurrection and Ascension. Third, Jesus promises that the powers of hell will never prevail over the Church. Since the Church is not simply a building, but rather the assembly of believers united in faith,[19] it follows that the only way the devil could destroy it would be through the introduction of theological error and heresy. Jesus' promise, therefore, amounts to a guarantee that the Church will never officially teach error in matters of faith and morals. Fourth, the "power of the keys" given to Peter signifies his God-given ability to make binding doctrinal decisions, as well as the power to forgive sins.[20]

PAPAL INFALLIBILITY

Sometimes the charism of papal infallibility is compared with the charism of biblical inspiration, which may be helpful as long as we realize that although they share similarities, they also have a major difference between them. Whereas the doctrine of biblical inspiration refers to a "positive" action of the Holy Spirit that empowered the sacred authors to write those things, and only those things, which God wanted, the charism of papal infallibility is a "negative" action of the Holy Spirit that prevents the pope from officially teaching error. The charism of papal infallibility prevents the possibility of error when the pope teaches a matter of faith or morals to be believed by the Universal Church. The pope, in making such pronouncements, cannot make new truth, but rather proclaims a truth that has always been believed in the history of the Church, but that may have been forgotten or neglected over time. It is important to recognize that papal infallibility pertains to the office[21] of the pope, and not to his person. We think of the examples in the history of the Church of popes who lived publicly wicked and immoral lives,[22] but never has there been a pope who

---

19 The primary function of a church building is to serve as the dignified gathering space for those who come to worship. In Communistic nations where churches are forbidden, Catholics gather secretly for the celebration of Mass. Although the church is the normative place for the celebration of Mass, the presence of a church (or even a building in general) is not essential for the celebration of the Holy Sacrifice of the Mass.

20 See Joseph Ratzinger, *Called to Communion* (San Francisco: Ignatius Press, 1996), 63–64.

21 "Office" refers to an official capacity.

22 The most infamous popes include Stephen VI (d. 897); Benedict IX (d. 1055 or 1056) and Alexander VI (d. 1503).

formally taught error.[23] The pope is a member of fallen humanity like the rest of us, and therefore does not cease to be a fallible, sinful man as an individual. The rectitude of his moral actions, thoughts, theological opinions, and teachings on issues other than faith or morals is not guaranteed by the charism of infallibility.

This charism of papal infallibility is also shared among the bishops in union with the pope, as taught by the Second Vatican Council's Dogmatic Constitution on the Church, also known as *Lumen gentium*:

> Although the individual bishops do not enjoy the prerogative of infallibility, they nevertheless proclaim Christ's doctrine infallibly whenever, even though dispersed through the world, but still maintaining the bond of communion among themselves and with the successor of Peter, and authentically teaching matters of faith and morals, they are in agreement on one position as definitively to be held. This is even more clearly verified when, gathered together in an ecumenical council, they are teachers and judges of faith and morals for the universal Church, whose definitions "must be adhered to with the obedience of faith."[24]

We observed early in this book that God was not content with simply prompting the sacred authors to write the Scriptures, but he also empowered them to affirm what He wanted communicated, nothing less and nothing more. We also discussed how the inerrancy of the Bible preserves the integrity and authority of the written Word. Similarly, Jesus promised to Peter that the gates of hell would never prevail over the Church,[25] yet if the pope were to teach moral or theological error to be obeyed by all the faithful, the Church would, in fact, be succumbing

---

23 Pope John XXII (d. 1334) incorrectly maintained that the souls of the deceased saints would not experience the Beatific vision until the Last Judgment; however, he made it clear that this was his personal opinion as a theologian. Papal infallibility does not prevent popes from holding false opinions about matters of faith or morals, but it does prevent a pope from formally teaching such false opinions as a matter of dogma to be held by the Universal Church.

24 CCC 891 and Second Vatican Council, *Lumen gentium*, no. 25.

25 See Matthew 16:18.

to the gates of hell. The charism of papal infallibility, therefore, was given by God so that it would be impossible for the pope to lead the people of God astray in matters of salvation.

There are two ways in which the pope directly exercises the charism of papal infallibility. The first way is through the "extraordinary" Magisterium, culminating in an *ex-cathedra* proclamation.[26] In Greek, a *kathedros* is a throne (hence a "cathedral," the mother church of a diocese, is the church that has the permanent "throne" or "chair" of the bishop). We recall that during the Middle Ages it was common for professors to teach sitting down, on their "chair" as a sign of authority. Similarly, an *ex-cathedra* ("from the throne") teaching of the pope is a solemn proclamation in matters of faith or morals that is clearly intended to be authoritative and binding upon the Catholic faithful throughout the world. Specific examples of papal infallibility being exercised in this way are the proclamations of the Immaculate Conception of Mary by Pope Pius IX in 1854, and that of the Assumption of Mary into heaven by Pope Pius XII in 1950.

The second way in which the pope may exercise the charism of papal infallibility is through the "ordinary" Magisterium. Again, the issue must be a matter of faith or morals to be held by the Universal Church, but instead of solemnly being proclaimed with much pomp and circumstance, these teachings are understood to be infallible insofar as they have been repeated by previous popes, or even strongly articulated by a single pope. A particularly relevant example of such infallible teaching through the ordinary Magisterium is the impossibility for a woman to receive Holy Orders, a teaching that is as ancient as the Church herself, which Pope John Paul II directly addressed in his Apostolic Letter of 1994, *Ordinatio sacerdotalis*:

> Wherefore, in order that all doubt may be removed regarding a matter of great importance, a matter which pertains to the Church's divine constitution itself, in virtue of my ministry of confirming the brethren (cf. Lk. 22:32) I declare that the Church has no authority whatsoever to confer priestly ordination on women

---

26 Second Vatican Council, *Lumen gentium*, no. 25.

and that this judgment is to be definitively held by all the Church's faithful.[27]

Since the pope is the pastor of the Universal Church and Vicar of Christ, Catholics are bound to accept the pope's teaching not only in matters infallibly defined (which are few), but in all matters of faith and morals, as taught by the Second Vatican Council:

> This religious submission of mind and will must be shown in a special way to the authentic Magisterium of the Roman Pontiff, even when he is not speaking *ex cathedra*; that is, it must be shown in such a way that his supreme Magisterium is acknowledged with reverence, the judgments made by him are sincerely adhered to, according to his manifest mind and will. His mind and will in the matter may be known either from the character of the documents, from his frequent repetition of the same doctrine, or from his manner of speaking.[28]

Conclusion

Unlike the Protestant denominations which accept only Scripture, and unlike the Orthodox Church which accepts only Scripture and Tradition, the Catholic Church looks to Scripture, Tradition, and the Magisterium as the means God gave to His Church to learn about Him. Under the governance of the Vicar of Christ, Catholics are able to learn the teachings of Christ and how they are to be lived out in the Christian life. Scripture, Tradition, and the Magisterium comprise the three legs of a theological tripod. Should any of these legs be knocked out, the whole truth about God as revealed in Jesus Christ is obscured and rendered inaccessible.

---

27 Pope John Paul II, Apostolic Letter On Reserving Priestly Ordination to Men Alone *Ordinatio sacerdotalis* (May 22, 1994), no. 4.
28 Second Vatican Council, *Lumen gentium*, no. 25.

Chapter 6

The Trinity and the Work of Creation

Overview

Of all the mysteries of the Catholic faith, there is one that is the most essential and fundamental: "The mystery of the Most Holy Trinity is the central mystery of Christian faith and life. It is the mystery of God in Himself. It is therefore the source of all the other mysteries of faith, the light that enlightens them. It is the most fundamental and essential teaching in the 'hierarchy of the truths of faith.'" (CCC 234). As a supernatural mystery of faith, the truth of the Trinity, unlike the truth of the existence of God, is utterly above the power of pure reason to comprehend. The only reason we know about the Trinity is because God communicated this truth to us through divine Revelation; had God not revealed this information to us, then no amount of brilliant thinking could ever have arrived at such knowledge.

The Trinity as Mystery

There is a legend told of St. Augustine walking on the beach and entering into a conversation with a young child. It was at the time in his life when he, as a prolific bishop, was writing his most difficult treatise of all, the treatise on the Most Holy Trinity. As he was thinking about the mystery of the Trinitarian God, he observed that this young boy on the beach was going back and forth from the ocean to a little hole in the sand while carrying a small seashell. Augustine approached the boy and asked him what he was doing, and the boy explained that he was going to take all of the water from the ocean and pour it using his seashell into the little hole that he had dug in the sand. Augustine was incredulous, pointing out to the boy that such a little hole could never contain the vastness of the ocean, to which the boy replied that in the same way, neither could a finite creature like Augustine ever comprehend the infinite mystery of the Trinity! Then the boy vanished and Augustine realized that it was really an angel with whom he had been conversing.

To talk about the Trinity is to refer to the fact of three persons[1] in one God. The three persons of the Trinity are known as the Father, the Son, and the Holy Spirit. These three persons all share the same divine nature,[2] yet they are not three separate gods, but together are one God. It is not correct to view the Father as a third part God, the Son as a third part God, and the Spirit as a third part God, because in God there are no parts. We can now begin to see how the Trinity is such a profound mystery.

There are many persons in history who have attempted to use some form of analogy to explain the relationship among the persons of the Trinity.[3] For example, consider the analogy using a three-leaved shamrock. Just as one leaf is made of three distinct leaflets, so too is there one God among a plurality of persons. Also consider an equilateral triangle; it is one geometric figure possessing three equal sides and three equal angles, just as there is one God, who exists as three equal persons. As a further example, consider the analogy of the family consisting of a husband, wife, and child. The three members constitute one family, illustrated through their common last name, and yet they also exist as distinct individuals, illustrated through their differing first names. Again it must be stressed that each of these analogies falls short of the

---

1   A person may be defined as an acting subject who is endowed with reason and free will. We acknowledge three types of persons: divine persons, angelic persons, and human persons.

2   A "nature" may be understood as a mode of operation. For example, as human persons we all share in one common human nature that we receive from our parents, which has been passed down from Adam.

3   Note that every analogy will always fall short of the reality, especially when God is the proper object of the analogy.

reality expressed, but they may help us to better apprehend the concept of what it means for there to be one [God] and yet three [persons] at the same time, but in different respects.

Although the term "Trinity" is not found in the Bible, an important principle to remember is that just because a word is not used (or in this case, even coined yet), it does not necessarily mean that the concept expressed by the word is not there. One of the clearest biblical passages in support of the Trinity is the baptismal formula given by Jesus to His apostles: "Go therefore and make disciples of all nations, baptizing them in the name of the Father and of the Son and of the Holy Spirit. . ." (Mt. 28:19). Note how Jesus does not tell His apostles to baptize in the *names* (plural) of the Father, and of the Son, and of the Holy Spirit, but in the *name* (singular) of the Father, and of the Son, and of the Holy Spirit. The baptism is made in the name of the one God, who exists as a plurality of three persons. As also can be inferred from this passage, each member of the Trinity is equal to the others, since each member is completely God. It is incorrect to claim that that Father is stronger than the Son, or that the Spirit knows more than the Father, or that the Son is more loving than the Spirit, etc.

Additionally, we must be careful not to read too much into some of the beautiful works of art that depict the Father as an old man with a beard and the Son as a younger man. It is understandable why this is done: the Father is made to be older because in human experience, a father is necessarily older than his son, but theologically this presentation is problematic. Since the Father and the Son (and everything said here also applies to the Holy Spirit) are equally God, then they must also be equally eternal (co-eternal), meaning that neither of them has a beginning in time. If God had a beginning in time, then some other being would have had to bring God into existence, meaning that God could not be God, since only God is the uncaused cause. If the Father and Son are co-eternal, neither one can be said to be "older" than the other.

The First Person of the Trinity

The first person of the Trinity is the Father, to whom is attributed the work of creation. Sometimes people may wonder why we call the Creator "Father," since there is no gender within the Trinity. For some, it seems to make sense to claim that since God the Creator is not male, but a pure, non-gendered Spirit, could not the first person of the Trinity be called "Mother" just as easily as "Father"? This line of argumentation especially resonates with some women who may have had very negative experiences in their relationship with their earthly fathers, and cannot bring themselves to see God in the same way.

Responding to this line of reasoning, we first observe that although the Creator is neither male nor female, we find within the Creator the perfection of all positive attributes common to both masculinity and femininity. Indeed the Creator is a strong protector, but also a loving nurturer. If we consider every possible positive attribute of both a father and a mother, we find all of them perfected in God as their source. So the question remains: Can the Creator be referred to as either Father or Mother? The answer is that the Creator may only be referred to as Father, and never as Mother. We shall explain.

To be a father means that one is the principle of generation of new life, and to be a mother means that one receives and nourishes the new life that has come into existence. Examples from biology are instructive: it is the man who transmits the seed, and the woman who receives that seed in order to bring about new human life. If God were mother instead of father, then God would have to wait until another source initiated the work of Creation, meaning that God would no longer be the Creator, nor the first principle of all things. "Father," therefore, is not simply a label affixed to our notion of the first person of the Trinity, but is the truth about God Himself. This is why Jesus clearly instructs us to pray to "Our *Father* who art in heaven. . ."[4] Additionally, recall the words of St. Paul to the Ephesians: "For this reason I bow my knees before the Father, from whom every family in heaven and on earth is named" (Eph. 3:14–15). In other words, we do not say that we first begin with our human experience of fatherhood, and then project that experience artificially onto God as "Father" in order to better relate to Him, but rather God's fatherhood metaphysically comes first, and then all human "fathers" are such insofar as they dimly participate in the fatherhood of almighty God.

---

4   See Matthew 6:9; Luke 11:2.

For those who do not like the idea of calling God "Father" due to negative situations that their own human fathers may have brought about, it is important to understand that doctrine cannot be changed due to pastoral concerns, no matter how sensitive and valid they may be. May they take great comfort in knowing that whereas their earthly father may have disappointed them, abandoned them, failed them, or even injured them, they have a true Father in heaven who will never fail, never leave them, and never stop loving them.

The Second Person of the Trinity

Although no Christian should be surprised that Jesus Christ is the second person of the Trinity, some Christians become surprised when they reflect that the person of Jesus Christ did not begin to exist at the moment of His conception in the womb of Mary, but rather pre-existed from all eternity as the eternal Word, the *Logos*. We already discussed in chapter one the meaning of the Greek term *logos* as a word, utterance, and principle of reason. When St. John writes in the prologue of his Gospel, "In the beginning was the Word, and the Word was with God, and the Word was God," he is referring to the second person of the Trinity, just as he also writes of Christ in the Book of Revelation: "He is clad in a robe dipped in blood, and the name by which he is called is The Word of God" (Rev. 19:13).

Consider the fact that you cannot know what I am thinking; however, if I speak to you, I am able to communicate via words content that is otherwise inaccessible to you. Words may therefore be said to be incarnate thoughts. The second person is called the Word (in the singular) for a specific reason:

> You recall that one and the same Word of God extends throughout Scripture, that it is one and the same Utterance that resounds in the mouths of all the sacred writers, since he who was in the beginning God with God has no need of separate syllables; for he is not subject to time.[5]

---

5   St. Augustine as quoted in CCC 102.

In sending us His Son, the Father exhausted everything that He could possibly say, since the Son is the perfect Revelation of the Father, lacking nothing. For this reason Jesus is not the "sentence" or the "paragraph" but rather the "Word" that is eternally generated from the Father, as we profess in the Creed. Hence Jesus Christ could truly say, "Have I been with you so long, and yet you do not know me. . . He who has seen me has seen the Father; how can you say, 'Show us the Father'? Do you not believe that I am in the Father and the Father in me?" (Jn. 14:9–10). Indeed the Father and the Son (as well as the Spirit) are all truly God and are equal in all ways. Their sole distinction is that they remain individual persons, albeit the same God.

Jesus Christ, the second person of the Trinity, is one divine person who bears two natures, both a divine nature and a human nature. Contrary to common expression, Jesus is not a *human* person, but rather a single *divine* person with both a human nature and a divine nature. Indeed the eternal Word took on a human nature and became like us in all things but sin;[6] however, He never ceased being a single divine person who existed as the *Logos* from all eternity. Jesus Christ is not 50 percent divine and 50 percent human, but as a divine person He is 100 percent true God and 100 percent true man.

The Third Person of the Trinity

The third person of the Trinity is known as the Holy Spirit, a name that reflects His sharing everything in common with both the Father and the Son, who are both supremely holy, and who are both Spirit (prior to the Incarnation of the Son). Just as in the Sacrament of Marriage where the love of husband and wife are meant to overflow into a child as the visible sign of the bond of love between the two parents, so too may the Holy Spirit be seen as the very bond of love between the Father and Son, a bond so strong that it is a person. Of course, with this type of analogy, one must recall that the Holy Spirit is indeed fully God, and therefore He is co-eternal with the Father and the Son. It would be an error to think of the Father as coming first, the Son as coming second, and then the Spirit as coming third. There never was a time when the Father, the Son, and the Holy Spirit did not exist; there never

---

6   See Hebrews 2:17 and 4:15.

was a time when any of the three persons of the Trinity was brought into existence.

The Sign of the Cross[7]

Pope Benedict XVI, writing as Joseph Cardinal Ratzinger, stated that "The most basic Christian gesture in prayer is and always will be the sign of the Cross,"[8] a gesture that contains within itself a high level of symbolism. First, consider that this sign is made in the shape of a Cross, which serves as a visible means of calling to mind our Lord's Passion and death through which He brought about our Redemption. At first, one may find it reprehensible to sign ourselves according to a form of execution; however, Jesus Christ embraced His death in order to give us life. The life that now comes from the Cross, the "original" tree of life once forfeited by Adam in Eden, is our focus, and not simply Jesus' death in itself. Second, the Sign of the Cross reminds us of our own baptism, when we (or our parents for us) chose to reject Satan and to embrace faith in Jesus Christ. Third, to make the Sign of the Cross is to place ourselves under the banner of Christ, thereby powerfully invoking God's protection. Fourth, the Sign of the Cross is a public profession of our belief in the Trinity. "Thus we can say that in the sign of the Cross, together with the invocation of the Trinity, the whole essence of Christianity is summed up. . ."[9]

The Work of Creation

Although the first person of the Trinity is attributed with the work of creation, the second person is attributed with the work of Redemption, and the third person attributed with the work of sanctification, each of the three divine persons is active in each of these roles. It would be incorrect to say that only the Father created all things, and only the Son redeemed us, and only the Holy Spirit sanctifies us. All three persons share the same divine nature and share in the same operation; indeed, "the whole divine economy is the common work of the three divine persons."[10]

---

7 This section borrows heavily from the insights offered by Joseph Ratzinger (Pope Benedict XVI) in his book, *The Spirit of the Liturgy* (San Francisco: Ignatius Press, 2000), 177–178.
8 Ibid., 177.
9 Ibid., 178.
10 See CCC 258.

God created all things *ex nihilo*, a Latin phrase meaning "out of nothing." God did not simply take pre-existing matter and mold it into something else (which is how one could define "to make"), but rather He brought something into being that did not exist in any way before (this is properly the meaning of "to create"). Only God is capable of creation in the strict sense; no other beings have such power.

Because everything that exists has its origin in God, it follows that all of creation is good. After the work of creation was finished, Scripture states, "And God saw everything that he had made, and behold, it was very good" (Gen. 1:31). If one were to posit that something in creation were evil, then it would mean that God created something that way, which contradicts the nature of God, and therefore is impossible.

What about the problem of evil? Consider that evil does not "exist" as a positive presence, but rather evil is the lack of the good that ought to be present. Hence we call evil a privation. Take for example the phenomenon of darkness. How does one define "darkness?" We do not define darkness according to what it is, but rather according to what it is not: darkness is the absence of light. In the same way, evil is not "something" at all, but rather the lack of "something" (i.e. the good) that ought to be present. There is not, nor could there ever be, something that is purely evil, since evil may be spoken of only in reference to the good that is presupposed.

Even in the extreme case of the devil, although he has freely chosen to renounce God and devote his existence to doing works of evil, the very existence of the devil is still fundamentally good. He was originally created by God, and like all living beings, he is also held in existence by God. Although he is indeed bent on evil, the devil can never become evil in his being. Perhaps we can state that the greatest irony concerning the devil is that although he spends his existence attempting to damn souls to hell in his unceasing hatred of God, his very being itself bears perpetual witness to the love of God who gave him life, and who continuously sustains him in being, knowing that His love will never be reciprocated.

Any proper understanding of the work of creation must necessarily include the truth of God's divine providence. God did not simply create the world and then leave it to run itself (like the "clockmaker" God of the Deists). "With creation, God does not abandon his creatures to themselves. He not only gives them being and existence, but also, at every moment, upholds and sustains them in being, enables them to act and brings them to their final end" (CCC 301). On the one hand, God respects free will, and on the other hand, nothing in the world could happen without God's knowledge and permission; such is how God wonderfully orders creation, always directly willing the good. In a later chapter we will further probe the problem of evil and suffering.

The Angels and Demons

Of all the things God created, we sometimes fail to consider the things that are invisible, but no less real, particularly the angels.[11] By definition, angels are non-corporeal persons who assist in God's governance of the world. The very term "angel" means "messenger" in Greek, denoting their important role as God's ambassadors.[12] Because they are non-corporeal, they are purely spiritual beings; this is why they are invisible. As persons, angels have an intellect and a will like humans do, however their intellects are vastly more powerful than ours. Contrary to a widely held misconception, angels are not human persons who have died. A human person cannot become an angel any more than a cat can become a human. We do not die and become angels, but we may die and become saints.

In the beginning, all the angels were created good, and then a number of them turned against God through the instigation of their leader, the devil, also known as Satan. The Fourth Lateran Council of the year 1215 taught, "For the devil and the other demons were indeed created by God naturally good, but they became evil by their own doing."[13] Those angels who turned from God became fallen angels, known as demons. Given the type of knowledge possessed by angels before their fall, the Church cites St. John Damascene in teaching: "It is the *irrevocable* character of their choice, and not a defect in the

---

11 It is noteworthy that the new English translation of the Creed no longer alludes to us believing in all things "seen and unseen" but rather "visible and invisible." This clarification points to the fact that indeed there exist real things that by their very nature are incapable of being seen, hence are said to be invisible, like angels, demons, and the human soul.

12 See CCC 328.

13 Denzinger 800; see also CCC 391.

infinite divine mercy, that makes the angels' sin unforgivable. 'There is no repentance for the angels after their fall, just as there is no repentance for men after death'" (CCC 393). There is never a possibility that the devil will be reconciled to God in the future, nor will there ever be a possibility that the angels who did not sin would later do so, since the angels were granted the beatific vision after they chose to remain faithful when the devil and his minions rebelled. Once a person (angel or human) enjoys the beatific vision in heaven, sin is impossible.

The proper view of angels is a balance between the extremes of materialism and the New Age movement. Materialism claims that only beings consisting of matter are truly real, and since angels do not consist of matter, the materialist concludes that such beings cannot exist. Materialism, therefore, denies the existence of angels. The New Age movement, on the other hand, elevates the importance of angels to the level of gods, effectively deifying them. The balanced view is that angels truly exist and participate in God's governance of the world, but they are not beings at the center of salvation history.

We all receive a guardian angel from God to help us in our spiritual fight against Satan during our earthly life. It would do us well to pray to the angels, especially to our guardian angel, for protection against the devil, and to ask St. Michael for the strength to be faithful to Christ in all things.

The Human Person

The creation of the human person marks the pinnacle of God's work of creation and the summit of the Creator's work.[14] Although there are several opinions as to how best to interpret the account of the creation of man and woman as conveyed in Genesis 1 and 2, there are two foundational theological principles that must be affirmed in order for the expressed opinion to be consistent with Catholic teaching. First, the immortal, spiritual, rational human soul could not have been the product of any evolutionary process, but necessarily infused directly by God into the first human. Second, every human person is biologically

---

14 See CCC 343.

descended from the first man, Adam, as our common father. As long as these two principles are preserved, then there is wide freedom in speculating about our origins, and even about theories of macro-evolution.[15]

Adam and Eve were the first two human persons. As human persons, we are a unity of both body and soul; to have one without the other renders us incomplete according to God's original plan. As a composite being of both body and soul, we cannot be reduced simply to our bodily and sensate dimension, nor can we be reduced simply to our soul and our spiritual dimension.

The higher powers of our soul include our intellect and our will. The intellect's job description is to seek the truth and to understand it, while the will's job description is to act upon the understanding we have gained through our intellect by choosing the good. We are able to know through our intellect, and we are able to choose through our will. Possessing the possibility of exercising both of these functions,[16] we are said to be made in God's image.[17] This is to say that the primary meaning of our "imaging" God has nothing to do with what we look like, since, prior to the Incarnation, the three persons of the Trinity remained purely spiritual and therefore without any physical appearance. We image God through our ability to know the truth and our ability to choose the good. Human persons and angelic persons are the only created beings in existence who are capable of truly knowing and choosing, and therefore both are rightly said to be created in the image of God. Our dignity, including the fact that a person may never be an object of use as a mere means to an end, is grounded in the fact that we are created in God's image, and nothing can ever blot out this image of God within us.

Our first parents lived in paradise, Eden, where there was no sin, and where they were immune from suffering and death. Living in intimate communion with God and with one another in the marital

---

15 See Pope Pius XII, Encyclical Letter on Concerning Some False Opinions *Humani generis* (August 12, 1950), nos. 36 and 37.

16 Possessing the possibility of using our intellect and will is not the same as actually using them. Therefore even those human beings who are unable to actually exercise their intellect and free will (a newly conceived child; very young children; very old persons who may have mental diseases, etc.) are still rightly said to be in God's image.

17 See Genesis 1:26.

covenant, they had everything they could ever hope for, and would have continued living in such a way if they had remained faithful to God. Due to their encounter with the devil and the poor decision they made, sin and death entered into human history, which we shall survey in the next chapter.

Conclusion

Belief in the Trinitarian God is an essential hallmark of Christianity, and perhaps no other gesture more fully summarizes the heart of the Christian faith than the Sign of the Cross accompanied by the invocation of the three persons of the Trinity. Out of an abundance of His love, God created heaven, earth, and all the creatures that populate them. Through pride, Satan and our first parents brought sin into the world, thereby rejecting the love of God that is at the heart of the work of creation and introducing moral evil into the world.

Chapter 7

Sin

Overview

Sin may be defined as an utterance, a deed, or a desire contrary to God's law,[1] which includes sins of commission as well as sins of omission. Whereas a sin of commission refers to something we do that we ought not to do, a sin of omission refers to us failing to do that which we ought. Sin represents a failure to love God, our neighbor, and ourselves, as Jesus teaches in His response to the question of which commandment is the most important: "You shall love the Lord your God with all your heart, and with all your soul, and with all your mind. This is the great and first commandment. And a second is like it, You shall love your neighbor as yourself. On these two commandments depend all the law and the prophets" (Mt. 22:37–40). The common denominator shared by both of these commandments is the commandment to love, and indeed these two commandments stand or fall together, since "If any one says, 'I love God,' and hates his brother, he is a liar; for he who does not love his brother whom he has seen, cannot love God whom he has not seen" (1 Jn. 4:20).

---

1   See CCC 1849.

Original Sin

It is not uncommon today for many Christians to be taught that Adam and Eve from the Book of Genesis simply did not exist. Yet Sacred Scripture of the Old and New Testaments, as well as the Catechism and the official teachings of both Judaism and Christianity, from the beginning have always affirmed the true existence of a historical Adam and Eve as the first parents of the human race. Although it is true that we do not know exactly how they came into being (a question pertaining to how literally the accounts of Genesis 1 and 2 are to be interpreted, which is beyond the scope of this chapter), it is absolutely true that they were the first human persons. Moreover, every human person is also biologically descended from them as Scripture teaches: "You made Adam and gave him Eve his wife as a helper and support. From them the race of mankind has sprung" (Tob. 8:6) and ". . . he made from one [man] every nation of men to live on all the face of the earth, having determined allotted periods and the boundaries of their habitation" (Acts 17:26). To deny that we are all biologically descended from a first set of parents (whom the Bible names Adam and Eve) is simply not a Christian option.

What were our first parents like? Adam and Eve each possessed an intellect that could immediately grasp the truth about life, and they each had a will that immediately carried out the good that corresponded to the truth understood through the intellect. They lived in paradise[2] in intimate communion with God, one another, and all of creation. But most importantly, they were created in the likeness of God. In the last chapter, we focused upon what it meant for Adam and Eve to be created in the image of God, and here we will focus upon what it meant to be created in the likeness of God. To be "God-like" is to be holy, and Adam and Eve lived in a state of sanctifying grace to the point that holiness itself could be said to be the very garment that clothed them. Sanctifying grace may be defined as that grace that makes us holy and pleasing to God. "Sanctifying grace is an habitual gift, a stable and supernatural disposition that perfects the soul itself to enable it to live with God, to act by his love" (CCC 2000). According to God's plan, their children, and their children's children, all the way down

---

2   The place "Eden" literally means "paradise."

to us today and beyond were meant to be born into this same type of paradise and to live in a state of harmony with God, neighbor, and all of creation. So what happened?

The devil made his entrance into human history.[3] Having already rejected God, Satan and his fellow rebellious angels were cast into hell and made it their primary purpose to lead as many humans into hell as possible until the end of the world. Appearing to Eve in the form of a serpent, Satan persuaded Eve to believe the lie that true happiness and freedom are to be found outside of communion with God. Satan purposely twisted God's words so that he sounded like an oppressive tyrant,[4] resulting in Eve's desire to distance herself from God so that she could make her own laws of good and evil instead of continuing to rely upon God.[5] Making the situation even more tragic, Eve promptly convinced her husband, Adam, to eat the forbidden fruit with her, resulting in the entrance of original sin into the world. "Man, tempted by the devil, let his trust in his Creator die in his heart and, abusing his freedom, disobeyed God's command. This is what man's first sin consisted of. All subsequent sin would be disobedience towards God and lack of trust in his goodness" (CCC 397). This first sin is called the "original" sin because it was the "first" transgression of the human race against God, a sin that had consequences not only for Adam and Eve, but for all of us as well. At the root of this sin is the same vice that is at the root of every sin: pride.[6]

---

3   Often it is incorrectly believed that the devil is the opposite of God. Consider that God is infinitely good, and since evil is a privation, there can never exist a being that is purely evil. Additionally, only God can be said to be infinite in any of His attributes. Recall from the previous chapter that the devil, also known as Satan, is a fallen angel. The opposite of Satan is St. Michael the Archangel, whom God commissions to send with His angelic armies against the powers of darkness.

4   Compare God's words given to Adam in Genesis 2:16–17 with Satan's version of them in Genesis 3:3. Note that God never said that they could not touch the tree; neither did God express His command in the negative as Satan does here. Additionally, Satan omits the fact that God told Adam that they could freely eat of every other tree in the Garden.

5   This is the meaning of Satan's words in Genesis 3:5, "For God knows that when you eat of it your eyes will be opened, and you will be like God, knowing good and evil." The sad irony is that Adam and Eve were already like God before the sin, and became alienated from Him and quite unlike Him through their sin.

6   Pride is the worst of the sins named the capital sins, of which the Catechism explains: "they are called 'capital' because they engender other sins, other vices" (1866). The seven capital sins are pride, avarice, envy, wrath, lust, gluttony, and sloth.

Once Adam and Eve sinned, their mode of existence entirely changed. First, they forfeited the life of sanctifying grace that they enjoyed up to this point, meaning that they spiritually died. The life of God they possessed within their souls was extinguished, and they no longer had a claim to eternal life. Whereas (we pointed out in the last chapter) we always remain in God's image, regardless of our choices in life, it is not true that the human person's likeness to God is a permanent attribute. From the moment of their sin, Adam and Eve ceased being like God. This was the most tragic effect of original sin.

A second effect of original sin is that the intellects of Adam and Eve became darkened in knowing the truth, and from this point onwards only with great difficulty could they understand the truth about themselves and the world in which they lived. A third effect is that their wills became weakened in choosing the good, so once they did arrive at a correct understanding of truth, their wills became hesitant to act promptly upon that truth so readily. A fourth effect of original sin is the introduction of disordered desires, including a basic inclination towards sin, which now required them to be on their guard and to fight against these disordered desires. This inclination is called concupiscence, which "unsettles man's moral faculties and, without being in itself an offense, inclines man to commit sins" (CCC 2515) and of which St. Paul states, "For I do not do the good I want, but the evil I do not want is what I do" (Rom. 7:19).[7] A final effect of original sin is that Adam and Eve became subjected to bodily death, a scenario that they could have avoided would they have remained faithful to God.

It is vital to understand that these effects of original sin did not simply apply to Adam and Eve, but they also affect all of us today. Why do these penalties incurred by Adam and Eve apply to us? Adam and Eve existed in a state of unfallen nature, but through their sin, known as "the Fall," their state of nature changed from unfallen nature to fallen nature.[8] We all exist as human persons in and through our common nature. Although there are approximately seven billion human persons in the world at this moment, there is only one common human nature that we all share. That nature we receive from our parents, who received

---

7   See also CCC 1264 and 1426.
8   See CCC 404.

it from their parents, all the way back to Adam.[9] If Adam had not sinned, and assuming for the moment that no human after Adam sinned, then we would all continue to exist in the same condition as Adam and Eve before their sin. Due to Adam's sin, however, the nature that all of his descendants (each of us) receive is wounded, fallen, and now subject to ignorance, weakness, concupiscence, and ultimately death itself.

At first glance, some might think that the inevitability of death is simply part of nature, and not specifically linked to any offense of God. The truth of the matter is that death is not natural. God created the human person in such a way that (through His supernatural gift of immortality) the human person would be immune from death.[10] Death was not in God's plan for Adam and Eve, nor was death in God's plan for any of us. Think about it this way: Would God really say to us, "I love you, but I am going to make sure that you suffer and die"? Death is a punishment due to sin. Consider the following two biblical passages that help to make this point clear. "God created man for incorruption, and made him in the image of his own eternity, but through the devil's envy death entered the world, and those who belong to his party experience it" (Wis. 2:23–24) and "Wherefore as by one man sin entered into this world and by sin death: and so death passed upon all men, in whom all have sinned" (Rom. 5:12, Douay). This understanding is explicit in the Church's teaching:

---

9   Genesis 5:1–3 states, "When God created man, he made him in the likeness of God. Male and female he created them, and he blessed them and named them Man when they were created. When Adam had lived a hundred and thirty years, he became the father of a son in his own likeness, after his image, and named him Seth" (emphasis added). Note that Adam was created in the likeness of God, and then Adam's son[s] come into being according to Adam's own image and likeness. Adam does still image God, so his offspring also image God, but Adam no longer is like God. Therefore the offspring of Adam and Eve, by being conceived in Adam's own likeness after the first sin, are not in God's likeness as Adam once was before his sin.

10   We must be careful to distinguish that, although we would all be immune from death if original sin had not occurred, we would still all be capable of death in the event of an accident, etc. In saying that the human person originally received the gift of immortality, we are not referring to an absolute understanding of immortality such as is true of the human soul.

Death is a consequence of sin . . . Even though man's nature is mortal, God had destined him not to die. Death was therefore contrary to the plans of God the Creator and entered the world as a consequence of sin. (CCC 1008)

Baptism provides the remedy for the *condition* of original sin, however there is no remedy for the *effects* of original sin: "Baptism, by imparting the life of Christ's grace, erases original sin and turns a man back toward God, but the consequences for nature, weakened and inclined to evil, persist in man and summon him to spiritual battle" (CCC 405).

Earlier it was pointed out that everything that exists is good, and therefore a newly conceived human person is good.[11] Due to the sin of Adam, however, newly conceived persons are not holy until they are baptized. Baptism fills the otherwise empty soul with the very life of God Himself through the infusion of sanctifying grace, thereby making the newly baptized person a new creation, a child of God and heir to heaven. St. Gregory of Nyssa offers the following beautiful reflection on Baptism: "Our spiritual birth is the result of a free choice, and we are in a certain way our own parents, creating ourselves as we wish ourselves to be, and through our will forming ourselves in accordance with the model that we choose."[12] Indeed, in the words of St. Gregory of Nazianzus, "Baptism is God's most beautiful and magnificent gift."[13]

Actual Sin

The Church teaches, "Although it is proper to each individual, original sin does not have the character of a personal fault in any of Adam's descendants" (CCC 405). This means that although we all are conceived in the state, or condition, of original sin, none of us are personally responsible for the sin, since original sin is contracted by propagation

---

11 We contrast this position with the erroneous opinion of the Protestant reformers, who taught that original sin did not simply wound man, but utterly depraved him, rendering him incapable of good works. See CCC 406.
12 St. Gregory of Nyssa, *The Life of Moses*, as cited by Pope Benedict XVI, General Audience of September 5, 2007.
13 See CCC 1216.

and not imitation. Actual sin, however, is that type of sin for which we are personally responsible, and this includes two kinds of actual sin distinguished according to their gravity: mortal sin and venial sin. The biblical foundation for such a distinction of sins can be found in 1 John 5:16–17: "If any one sees his brother committing what is not a mortal sin, he will ask, and God will give him life for those whose sin is not mortal. There is sin which is mortal; I do not say that one is to pray for that. All wrongdoing is sin, but there is sin which is not mortal."

Coming from the Latin term for "death," mortal sins alienate us from the life of God; in theological terms, the commission of a mortal sin causes us to lose the state of sanctifying grace, meaning that if we died in such a condition, we would go immediately to hell.

> Mortal sin is a radical possibility of human freedom, as is love itself. It results in the loss of charity and the privation of sanctifying grace, that is, of the state of grace (CCC 1861) . . . To die in mortal sin without repenting and accepting God's merciful love means remaining separated from him for ever by our own free choice. This state of definitive self-exclusion from communion with God and the blessed is called "hell." (CCC 1033)

What are the essential components of a mortal sin? "Mortal sin is sin whose object is grave matter and which is also committed with full knowledge and deliberate consent."[14] Each of the Ten Commandments expresses grave obligations and therefore it is possible to sin mortally against the subject matter of any one of the Ten Commandments.[15] The three conditions for committing a mortal sin make it clear that it is impossible to commit a mortal sin by accident. Given that the commission of one mortal sin is sufficient to send the sinner to hell for all eternity, it makes sense that a mortal sin must be intentional as such.

If at least one of the three criteria for the commission of a mortal sin is lacking, then the result is called a venial sin, also known as a "small"

---

14 Pope John Paul II, Apostolic Exhortation on Reconciliation and Penance *Reconciliatio et paenitentia* (December 2, 1984), no. 12; see also CCC 1857.

15 See CCC 2072.

or "slight" sin. Venial sin constitutes an offense against God, but the gravity of this sin is insufficient to break our relationship with Him. Although such sins do not break our relationship with God, they still represent a failure to love, and an increase in venial sins makes more likely the possibility that we will commit a mortal sin.[16] Sometimes persons dismiss venial sins, claiming that it does not really matter if one commits such small sins, as long as one stays away from serious sins. That perspective fails to take into account that since every sin offends God in some way, and since God is infinite, it can be said that even small sins represent an infinite offense against God.

While it is true that venial sins will not send a person to hell, it is equally true that such sins can prevent a person from entering heaven for a long time after death.[17] Additionally, the "childish" motive for avoiding sins is often due to fear of punishment, and since venial sins do not incur the punishment of damnation, people may not take these sins seriously. However, the mature motive for avoiding sins is not because we fear punishment (focus is on the self), but rather because we love God and know that we always need to follow His example of charity. This latter view constitutes perfect contrition, and ought to be a driving principle in our lives.

Once a mortal sin is committed, Catholics are obliged to make use of the wonderful Sacrament of Reconciliation (also called Penance or Confession) to be forgiven of that sin. "Thus it follows that all mortal sins of which penitents after a diligent self-examination are conscious must be recounted by them in confession, though they may be most secret and may have been committed only against the last two precepts of the Decalogue [cf. Ex 20:17; Deut 5:21; Mt 5:28]; for these sins sometimes wound the soul more grievously and are more dangerous than those that are committed openly."[18] The principle is simple to understand, even if difficult to live: if a person is truly sorry for his grave offense against God, then he will make use of the very means instituted by God for the forgiveness of such sin. If the person refuses, then it reveals that the person cannot be truly sorry for the sin in the first place.

---

16 See CCC 1863.
17 This concept will be addressed in the last chapter.
18 Denzinger, 1680.

Concerning only venial sins, the Sacrament of Reconciliation is not strictly required for the forgiveness of these sins, although it is highly recommended.[19] While it is true that the Sacrament of Reconciliation was primarily instituted for the forgiveness of mortal sins committed after baptism, and that we are only bound to confess mortal sins, it is also extremely helpful for the spiritual life to confess venial sins. The reason for this practice rests in an understanding of the sacraments: the sacraments are extensions of God's power into our lives, and by confessing venial sins through the Sacrament of Reconciliation instead of simply praying for forgiveness in the privacy of our room, not only do we receive the forgiveness of these sins, but we also are given the added sacramental graces that strengthen us to avoid sin in the future. In a time when we have largely lost the sense of sin, we do ourselves more good than we know by making frequent recourse to the Sacrament of Reconciliation.[20] God's mercy is endless. He does not place a limit on forgiveness, even for the most hardened of sinners who may have spent an entire lifetime doing wicked deeds. As long as the sinner is truly sorry for the sins committed and is prepared to make amends for the wrongdoing, God can and will forgive these sins.

It is sometimes asked whether it is true that God is willing to forgive every sin, since the Bible clearly makes reference to an unforgiveable sin: "Therefore I tell you, every sin and blasphemy will be forgiven men, but the blasphemy against the Spirit will not be forgiven. And whoever says a word against the Son of man will be forgiven; but whoever speaks against the Holy Spirit will not be forgiven, either in this age or in the age to come" (Mt. 12:31–32). The Church understands this teaching to relate to the specific sin of final impenitence, which is a particular sin against the Holy Spirit. The sin of final impenitence means that the sinner is not sorry for his sins, and therefore is not willing to ask God for forgiveness. A person who dies in this spiritual condition cannot be saved. As can be seen, this teaching does not contradict the fact that God will forgive every sin of ours for which we are truly sorry and have firm purpose of amendment.

---

19 See CCC 1458.

20 As an Archbishop, the future Pope John Paul II went to Confession every week. See Stanislaw Cardinal Dziwisz, *A Life With Karol* (New York: Doubleday, 2007), 11. For most Catholics who are actively seeking to do the Lord's will, Confession about every three weeks is appropriate, unless mortal sin is committed in which case one should go promptly.

One of the most profound teachings of Jesus concerning the Sacrament of Confession is the parable[21] of the Prodigal Son, found in the fifteenth chapter of the Gospel of Luke. This chapter consists of three parables of God's mercy: the lost sheep; the lost coin; and the lost (prodigal) son. This last parable shall be our focus below, a parable that not only details the situation of the lost son, but also highlights the love and mercy of his father. For these reasons the parable of the prodigal son can equally be called the parable of the merciful father, and the details provided about the prodigal son relate to each one of us as we continue the life-long work of conversion.[22]

There are two sons in this parable; however, for our purposes we shall only focus upon the younger son. This younger son said to his father, "give me the share of property that falls to me." Normally, it would be at the father's death that the sons would receive their inheritance; therefore this request of the younger son is akin to saying, "You mean nothing to me; die now and give me what is mine." The son's demand is a self-centered desire for complete independence from his father, which becomes the situation of each one of us every time we choose to sin against God. The younger son then went into a far country, and there squandered his property in loose living, which reminds us of the fact that whenever we commit serious sin, we bring ourselves far away from our heavenly Father and lose our true purpose in life. When we have alienated ourselves from God in this manner, all we have left are fleeting distractions that can never compensate for the absence of God. We further read that "when he had spent everything, a great famine arose in that country, and he began to be in want," signaling that the situation has turned desperate. Indeed once all the "toys" of life disappear, we are forced to face our sins and recognize the deep hunger within us for truth and goodness that only God can satisfy.

---

21 A parable is a short, fictitious story that is intended to communicate a moral lesson. Jesus often taught in parables as a way of ensuring that even the simple and uneducated persons among Him could understand Him.

22 "That son, who receives from the father the portion of the inheritance that is due to him and leaves home to squander it in a far country 'in loose living,' in a certain sense is the man of every period, beginning with the one who was the first to lose the inheritance of grace and original justice. The analogy at this point is very wide-ranging. The parable indirectly touches upon every breach of the covenant of love, every loss of grace, every sin" (Pope John Paul II, Encyclical Letter on the Mercy of God *Dives in misericordia* [November 13, 1980], no. 5).

The parable continues, "He went and joined himself to one of the citizens of that country, who sent him into his fields to feed swine. And he would gladly have fed on the pods that the swine ate; and no one gave him anything." The younger son gets a job feeding pigs, which were unclean animals for a Jew, symbolizing his unclean and immoral spiritual state. In this lowest state, he thinks to himself, "How many of my father's hired servants have bread enough and to spare, but I perish here with hunger! I will arise and go to my father, and I will say to him, 'Father, I have sinned against heaven and before you; I am no longer worthy to be called your son; treat me as one of your hired servants.'" Resolutely, the wayward son arose and began the journey back to his father. We reflect on how the son "came to himself," i.e. he acknowledged his sin and was determined to seek forgiveness from his father whom he offended. He decided to go before his father and throw himself on his father's mercy, knowing that it is better to be a servant in the house of his father than be free in this far away land. He was prepared to accept the consequences of deep humiliation and shame, thereby manifesting his true contrition and becoming a living witness of the truth taught by St. John concerning our relationship with our heavenly Father, "If we say we have no sin, we deceive ourselves, and the truth is not in us. If we confess our sins, he is faithful and just, and will forgive our sins and cleanse us from all unrighteousness" (1 Jn. 1:8–9).

Although one may expect the parable to end here with the son's steadfast decision to return to his father and beg for mercy, it unexpectedly transitions to a second part that draws attention to the merciful love of the father. We are told that as the son journeyed home, his father saw him from a distance, which suggests that the father must have been waiting for him and searching for his son. Upon seeing him, the father, who was the one deeply offended, did not wait for the son to come to him, but rather took the initiative to run out to meet him. This is always God's attitude towards us when we repent from our sins. Indeed the father realized that, although the son squandered the material inheritance, he saved the one thing that really matters, namely, his soul. Faithful to his promise, the son said to his father, "Father, I have sinned against heaven and before you; I am no longer worthy to be called your son." Unexpectedly, the father responds by putting a robe, ring, and sandals on his son. The cloak is a sign that the son's innocence is restored and is a symbol of his restored sanctifying grace.[23] The ring is a sign of honor and authority, and that he was given sandals alludes to the end of his period of servitude to sin, since slaves commonly went barefoot. Collectively, the cloak, ring, and sandals represent the restoration of the son to the family. In celebration of the sinner's return home, the father calls for a feast that represents the Eucharist. Summarizing this high point of the parable, Pope John Paul II reflects, "The most striking element of the parable is the father's festive and loving welcome of the returning son: It is a sign of the mercy of God, who is always willing to forgive. Let us say at once: Reconciliation is principally a gift of the heavenly Father."[24]

Conclusion

Indeed "Scripture and the Church's Tradition continually recall the presence and *universality of sin in man's history*" (CCC 401) while at the same time constantly urging us to "fight the good fight of the faith" (1 Tim. 6:12). with the help of divine grace. Although Baptism removes the condition of original sin, we are constantly tempted to personal sin through the powers of concupiscence working within us. With the aid of the sacraments of the Church, especially Reconciliation and the Eucharist, we are able to persevere on our journey to heaven. As illustrated through the parable of the Prodigal Son, God is always waiting for our return when we have alienated ourselves from Him due to grave sin, and He will welcome us back with open arms if we only express true sorrow for our sin and avail ourselves to His mercy and forgiveness through the sacrament of Confession.

---

23 Earlier it was pointed out that Adam and Eve could be said to "wear" sanctifying grace like a coat prior to their sin, and that when they did sin, they lost this "garment" of sanctifying grace. Here in the parable of the Prodigal Son, we are told that the father gave his son the *protos stole*, literally meaning the "first coat," thereby forging a link back to the first coat of sanctifying grace which covered Adam and Eve.
24 Pope John Paul II, *Reconciliatio et paenitentia*, no. 5.

Chapter 8

The Incarnation and the Work of Redemption

Overview

The term "incarnation" comes from Latin and literally means "the action of becoming in-fleshed." It refers to the fact that the Eternal Word (the Logos), the Second Person of the Blessed Trinity, took on a true human nature in the womb of His mother, Mary. Contrary to common opinion, the event of the Incarnation did not take place on Christmas, but rather with the Annunciation,[1] since it was in the context of the Annunciation to Mary that the Eternal Word took on a true human nature.[2]

The Catechism provides four reasons for the Incarnation: First, in order for God to save us from sin by reconciling us with Himself; second, so that we would know God's love; third, that Jesus would be our model of holiness; and fourth, that we may be made partakers of the divine nature, according to the words of St. Athanasius, "For the Son of God became man so that we might become God."[3] Of course, this statement of St. Athanasius cited in the Catechism (460) does not imply that we "turn into God," but it refers to the fact that a person in the state of grace is said to be *divinized*, that is, becoming God-like through sharing in His divine grace.

---

1   The Solemnity of the Annunciation is liturgically celebrated on March 25th.
2   See Luke 1:26–38.
3   See CCC 456–460.

The unique and altogether singular event of the Incarnation of the Son of God does not mean that Jesus Christ is part God and part man, nor does it imply that He is the result of a confused mixture of the divine and the human. He became truly man while remaining truly God, thus being true God and true man. During the first centuries, the Church had to defend and clarify this truth of faith against the many heresies that falsified it through denying either Jesus' true humanity or His true divinity, thereby obscuring the full truth of the Incarnation. Some of the more significant of these heresies are Docetism, Adoptionism, Arianism, Apollinarianism, Nestorianism,[4] Monophysitism and Monothelitism.

Docetism

The heresy of Docetism, championed by the Manichean and Gnostic sects, denied Jesus' true humanity, because it was believed by some that matter was evil and therefore unworthy to be united to God. The Docetists claimed that Jesus *appeared* to be man and *appeared* to suffer and die, but never really did. The Church responded by pointing out that if Jesus Christ did not really suffer and die for us while truly man, then we are not truly redeemed, as highlighted by the teaching of St. Gregory Nazianzus: "What has not been assumed has not been healed."[5] One of the earliest defenders of the true faith against the Docetist heresy was St. Ignatius of Antioch (d. 107), who wrote the following as he was being led to his martyrdom:

> But if, as some that are without God, that is, the unbelieving, say, He became man in appearance [only], that He did not in reality take unto Him a body, that He died in appearance [merely], and did not in very deed suffer, then for what reason am I now in bonds, and long to be exposed to the wild beasts? In such a case, I die in vain, and am guilty of falsehood against the Cross of the Lord.[6]

---

4 The heresy of Nestorianism will be discussed again in the next chapter.
5 Cited by Pope Benedict XVI, General Audience of August 22, 2007.
6 Letter to the Trallians, chapter 10, *The Ante-Nicene Fathers*, Vol. 1 (Grand Rapids: Eerdmans), 70.

The testimony of Scripture clearly refutes the errors of Docetism. For example, we read "the Word became flesh and dwelt among us" (Jn. 1:14), which excludes every possibility of a merely simulated union between the Word and humanity. Additionally, the risen Jesus invites Thomas to put his fingers through His nail wounds precisely to prove that He is real,[7] further inviting His apostles, "See my hands and my feet, that it is I myself; handle me, and see; for a spirit has not flesh and bones as you see that I have" (Lk. 24:39).

Remnants of this heresy are found in today's culture within those who show a disdain for the body, expressing a devaluation of the human body and human sexuality. It is also exhibited by those who view the body simply as a "chain of the soul" and who falsely think that our body is nothing more than temporary, earthly baggage from which the soul yearns to be free.

Adoptionism

The heresy of Adoptionism, spread by Paul of Samosata (d. 272), denied that Jesus was truly the Son of the Father by nature, claiming that Jesus became the Son of God through adoption. If this position were true, Jesus' relationship to the Father would not be essentially different than the relationship of any baptized person to the Father. It would also be akin to the situation of a child today who is adopted into a family and becomes a true member of that family, but who is not the natural child of his new parents.

Some proponents of this heresy claimed that this adoption took place when Jesus was baptized, while others maintained that it happened only with Jesus' Resurrection. Regardless, this heresy clearly denies the true divinity of Jesus Christ and is at odds with passages in Scripture that point to a clear relationship between the Father and Son by their very common divine nature, thereby opposing any Adoptionist influences. Consider the following two biblical passages: "No one has ever seen God; the only Son, who is in the bosom of the Father, he has made him known" (Jn. 1:18) and "for God so loved the world that he gave his only Son, that whoever believes in him should not perish but have eternal life" (Jn. 3:16). These passages reaffirm the natural filiation of the Son, thereby excluding theories of Adoptionism.

---

7   See John 20:25–29.

Today echoes of this heresy are found in those who consider Jesus merely a good person; simply a valiant social reformer; a holy person who had a strong bond and relationship with God, much like the greatest saints of Christianity and other strong religious figures of other faith traditions.

Arianism

The Arian heresy was an extremely widespread heresy that even infected many priests and bishops, requiring much effort by the Church to stamp out. Arius (d. circa 336) was a priest of Alexandria who, in an attempt to underscore the majesty of God, believed that the Word of God, the Logos, was neither eternal nor divine, but itself a creation, albeit the most excellent creation, of the Father. He reasoned that if God is truly Father, and since in our experience every father necessarily pre-exists his son, it followed that there was a time when the Father existed apart from the Son, and therefore a time when the Son was not.[8]

Statements found in Scripture like "I and the Father are one" (Jn. 10:30) and "Do you not believe that I am in the Father, and the Father in me" (Jn. 14:10) were manipulated by Arius in such a way that it became virtually impossible to convince him of the error of his views.

Normally, theological disputes could be addressed at the local level, but Arius' beliefs quickly began to divide Catholics, with many priests and bishops coming to his defense to the point that local synods came to opposing conclusions, with some favoring Arianism and others rejecting it. Given the grand scale of the dispute, the Holy Roman Emperor Constantine intervened and called the first ecumenical council of the Catholic Church in order to prevent a massive schism within the Empire, which would bring both theological and political disorder. This Council summoned in the year 325 is known as the Council of Nicaea.

The bishops at Nicaea overwhelmingly agreed to the true understanding of Christ's relation to the Father, and the Greek term *homoousios* (which means, "of the same substance") was employed to settle the controversy, preserving the substantial unity of the Father and the Son

---

8 See CCC 465.

over and against Arius' claim.[9] The Niceno-Constantinopolitan Creed, which we profess each Sunday bears witness to this victory over the Arian heresy. Consider the following reflections of Pope Benedict XVI:

> In this fundamental text—which expresses the faith of the undivided Church and which we also recite today, every Sunday, in the Eucharistic celebration—the Greek term *homooúsios* is featured, in Latin *consubstantialis*: it means that the Son, the Logos, is "of the same substance" of the Father, he is God of God, he is his substance. Thus, the full divinity of the Son, which was denied by the Arians, was brought into the limelight.[10]

It is interesting that a non-biblical term was used to resolve (at least initially) this early Christological controversy at a time when all of theology still heavily revolved around Scripture. It is also indicative of the movement of the early Church beyond solely Judaic ways of thinking, making use of the vast contributions of Greek philosophy in service to theology. Benedict XVI's reflections are pertinent here: He comments that the word *homoousios* is the only philosophical term that was incorporated into the Creed, and yet this term functions to safeguard the reliability of the biblical term that identifies what it means for Jesus to be the Son of the Father.[11]

Apollinarianism

Begun by Apollinarius (d. 390), the heresy of Apollinarianism maintained that Jesus did not have a human soul, because Apollinarius falsely claimed that it was absorbed by the Logos in virtue of the Incarnation. Yet we may ask that if Jesus truly became man, a truth that Apollinarius accepted, how could He have done so without uniting Himself to the noblest part of the human being? It would not be possible for Jesus to have become fully human without having a human soul, since the soul is an essential dimension of humanity.

---

9   It should be noted that the full implications of the term *homoousios* were not finally understood and accepted until the First Council of Constantinople in 381, largely through the efforts of St. Athanasius.

10 Pope Benedict XVI, General Audience of June 20, 2007.

11 See Pope Benedict XVI, *Jesus of Nazareth*, 320.

Furthermore, consider that the intellect and will are both powers of the soul, and it is through our intellect and will that we freely choose to sin. It is unreasonable to consider that God became man to save us from sin, and yet chose not to unite Himself to the very place where sin begins in order to purify and elevate it.

Apollinarianism was officially condemned at the First Council of Constantinople in 381.

Nestorianism

In the 5th century, the patriarch of Constantinople, Nestorius (d. 451), argued that Mary cannot be called the Mother of God (*theotokos*), but only the Mother of Christ (*Christotokos*). Nestorius maintained that God did not really become man, but that God dwelt within the man called Jesus in a manner similar to the way God is said to dwell within a temple. He thought that there were two persons in Jesus, rather than one person with two natures.

The third ecumenical council of the Church, the Council of Ephesus (431), formally condemned the position of Nestorius in twelve canons formulated by St. Cyril of Alexandria (d. 444), who presided over the Council.

Monophysitism

Introduced by a monk named Eutyches, the Monophysite (literally, "one nature") heresy was a reaction to Nestorianism that went too far: it denied that the human nature of Jesus remained once the Logos assumed it. The Monophysites thought that somehow the divine nature absorbed the human nature, resulting in only one nature in Christ, a nature that was neither truly divine nor truly human. The Council of Chalcedon in 451, the fourth ecumenical council of the Church, responded to the Monophysite claim in teaching:

> We confess that one and the same Lord Jesus Christ, the only begotten Son, must be acknowledged in two natures, without confusion or change, without division or separation. The distinction between the natures was never abolished by their union but rather the character

proper to each of the two natures was preserved as they came together in one Person. . .[12]

Monothelitism

The heresy of Monothelitism (literally, "one will") affirmed against the Monophysites that Jesus had two natures, however they wrongly maintained that Jesus only had one divine will, with only a divine mode of operation. This position was condemned at the Third Council of Constantinople (680–681): "And so we proclaim two natural wills in Him, and two natural operations indivisibly, inconvertibly, inseparably, unfusedly. . . . in our Lord Jesus Christ Himself, our true God, that is, the divine operation and the human operation. . ."[13]

The Work of Redemption

Now that we have probed the full truth about the Incarnation, the issue of the purpose of the Incarnation can be addressed. The Son of God became man in order to die for us, offering His life as a sacrifice to redeem[14] us from our sins and to lead us to heaven. Everything Jesus did was ultimately ordered to the Cross, which would become both the instrumental cause and perpetual sign of our salvation. By exploring the sacrifice of Jesus, we can grow in our awareness of the gratitude we owe to almighty God, and we can discern the significance of suffering in our own lives as we continue our pilgrimage of faith towards heaven.

When we consider the death of Jesus, we must not begin with the assumption that Jesus was put to death as a result of the strength of His enemies compared to His human weakness. This passive view of Jesus' death is in error. The truth is that He was actively in control of the whole event of His suffering and death from its beginning until its end. Jesus' life was not passively taken from Him, but actively offered up for our sakes. Consider John 10:14–15: "I am the good shepherd; I know my own and my own know me, as the Father knows me and I know the Father; and I lay down my life for the sheep" in conjunction

---

12 Denzinger, 302. See also CCC 467.
13 Definition of the Two Wills of Christ, Denzinger 291.
14 The word "redemption" means "to ransom; to buy back," i.e. Jesus frees us from bondage to sin by cancelling our punishment due to sin.

with John 10:17–18, "For this reason the Father loves me, because I lay down my life, that I may take it again. No one takes it from me, but I lay it down of my own accord. I have power to lay it down, and I have power to take it again; this charge I have received from my Father." Both priest and victim, Jesus was a willing sacrifice.

Considering those responsible for Jesus' death, we make a distinction between Jesus' death understood as a *historical* event, and Jesus' death understood as a *theological* event. Understood as a historical event, the majority (though not all) of the Jewish leaders living at the time of Jesus who found Him guilty of blasphemy[15] and handed Him over to the Romans were mainly responsible for His death. Recall that the Jews were living under the authority of the Roman Empire, and thus the Jewish people had no authority to put anyone to death, even though the Old Testament law demanded it in several instances, including the crime of blasphemy.[16]

Since the Jews could not execute Jesus for blasphemy, they devised a way for the Romans to do it through the charge of treason, which amounts to the claim that Jesus was a self-appointed king of the Jews, and therefore a rival to the Emperor. Thus the majority of Jewish leaders as well as a number of Romans are responsible for the death of Jesus when it is understood as a historical event.

At the heart of Jesus' death, however, is its theological significance. When we consider Jesus' death as a theological event, it follows that *all of us* are guilty of the death of Jesus because He died to redeem us all from our sins. It is not appropriate to point the finger at the number of Jews who put Him to death, nor to the Romans who cooperated with His death, but we must point our finger back at ourselves. As St. Francis of Assisi has said, "Nor did demons crucify him; it is you who have crucified him and crucify him still, when you delight in your vices and sins."[17] From the Cross, Jesus cried out concerning the Romans and the

---

15 "Blasphemy . . . consists in uttering against God—inwardly or outwardly—words of hatred, reproach, or defiance" (CCC 2148). The Jews considered Jesus' claim to divinity to be false, and therefore blasphemous.

16 Leviticus 24:16 states, "He who blasphemes the name of the LORD shall be put to death; all the congregation shall stone him; the sojourner as well as the native, when he blasphemes the Name, shall be put to death."

17 As cited in CCC 598.

Jews of His time, "Father, forgive them; for they know not what they do" (Lk. 23:34), and Peter affirmed, "And now, brethren, I know that you acted in ignorance, as did also your rulers" (Acts 3:17). But the same cannot be said of us today: When we sin, we do not do so out of ignorance, but through deliberately defying the love of almighty God.

Unfortunately, some people today still view the Jewish people as 'Christ killers' and accuse them of the death of Jesus Christ. Concerning this, the Second Vatican Council taught the following:

> True, the Jewish authorities and those who followed their lead pressed for the death of Christ; still, what happened in His passion cannot be charged against all the Jews, without distinction, then alive, nor against the Jews of today. Although the Church is the new people of God, the Jews should not be presented as rejected or accursed by God, as if this followed from the Holy Scriptures.[18]

It would serve us well to remember that God never revoked the covenants He made with the Jewish people, and the Jewish people retain a most privileged place in salvation history, as alluded to by St. Paul: "They are Israelites, and to them belong the sonship, the glory, the covenants, the giving of the law, the worship, and the promises; to them belong the patriarchs, and of their race, according to the flesh, is the Christ, who is God over all, blessed forever. Amen" (Rom. 9:4–5). And a little later he adds, "I ask, then, has God rejected his people? By no means! I myself am an Israelite, a descendant of Abraham, a member of the tribe of Benjamin. God has not rejected his people whom he foreknew" (Rom. 11:1–2).[19]

---

18 Second Vatican Council, Declaration on the Relations of the Church to Non-Christian Religious *Nostra aetate* (October 28, 1965), no. 4.

19 It is extremely important that one reads the Letter to the Romans as a whole, especially chapters 9–11, lest one manipulate Paul's teaching by taking a few passages out of their proper context in order to assert that God did, indeed, annul His covenant with the Jewish people and withdraw His love from them. The full reading of Romans reveals quite the opposite interpretation, which is the position advanced by the Church.

Redemptive Suffering

Suffering is almost inseparable from man's earthly existence; it is universal, and it is something that we naturally seek to avoid or at least to lessen. In relation to suffering, some people wonder what the expression "offer it up" is all about, and many people wonder why an all-good God allows the innocent to suffer. Others are curious about why Catholics have crucifixes depicting the suffering Jesus in our churches and around our necks, while Protestants have only empty crosses.[20] To respond to these questions, we must probe the mystery of suffering.

Pope John Paul II had extremely valuable insights into the mystery of suffering. He not only wrote as pope, but as a man who himself was no stranger to intense emotional, physical and spiritual suffering throughout his lifetime. His mother died before he reached the age of nine, and his older brother, a medical doctor, died just three years later from exposure to scarlet fever after he treated an afflicted patient.[21] He was twenty when his father died, and he lived under the persecution of both Communism and Nazism. He was nearly assassinated on May 13, 1981, being struck by two bullets, the first piercing his abdomen, colon, and small intestines, and the second breaking his left index finger. He was rushed to the hospital in an ambulance with broken sirens, in order to receive a blood transfusion that proved unsuccessful, resulting in the doctors themselves providing their own blood for the new, successful transfusion.[22] He met with his would-be assassin Mehmet Ali Agca soon after his recovery, thinking that the man wanted to seek forgiveness from him, only to be told, "I know I was aiming right. I know that the bullet was a killer. So why aren't you dead?"[23] Just a year later, he was stabbed by one of his own priests while he went to Fatima in thanksgiving for the preservation of his life the year before. He realized in 1991 that he was developing Parkinson's disease, and he personally struggled with the question of whether he should resign the papacy once he reached eighty years old in 2000.[24] He ultimately

---

20 A crucifix has the body of Jesus on it, while a cross does not.
21 George Weigel, *Witness to Hope* (Harper Perennial: New York, 2005), 32.
22 Stanislaw Cardinal Dziwisz, *A Life With Karol*, 131–133.
23 Ibid., 137.
24 Ibid., 221–222.

died on the vigil of Divine Mercy Sunday, a feast that he himself instituted, becoming a witness in his very person to the salvific meaning of human suffering.

Pope John Paul II reflected:

> Suffering seems to be particularly *essential to the nature of man*. It is as deep as man himself, precisely because it manifests in its own way that depth which is proper to man, and in his own way surpasses it. Suffering seems to belong to man's transcendence: it is one of those points in which man is in a certain sense "destined" to go beyond himself, and he is called to do this in a mysterious way.[25]

Granted that Christ's Redemption does not obliterate or even lessen our suffering in the world, what it does do is provide the meaning, a reason, for human suffering, and an understanding of its great value for the spiritual life. Through our suffering, we are able to realize our weakness and inadequacies, and as John Paul wrote, it allows us:

> to become particularly *susceptible*, particularly *open to the working of the salvific powers of God*, offered to humanity in Christ. . . . When this body is gravely ill, totally incapacitated, and the person is almost incapable of living and acting, all the more do interior *maturity and spiritual greatness* become evident, constituting a touching lesson to those who are healthy and normal.[26]

John Paul II further observed, "In the Cross of Christ not only is the Redemption accomplished through suffering, but *also human suffering itself has been redeemed*."[27] Christ raises human suffering to the level of the redemption, and insofar as we suffer, we can become a sharer in the redemptive suffering of Christ. For this reason, one can speak of

---

25 Pope John Paul II, Apostolic Letter on the Christian Meaning of Human Suffering *Salvifici doloris* (February 11, 1984), no. 2.

26 Ibid., nos. 23 and 26.

27 Ibid., no. 19.

a certain joy and peace to be found in suffering when viewed through the eyes of faith. This teaching is strongly found in Pauline texts of the New Testament. Consider the following excerpts:

> Therefore, since we are justified by faith, we have peace with God through our Lord Jesus Christ. Through him we have obtained access to this grace in which we stand, and we rejoice in our hope of sharing the glory of God. More than that, we rejoice in our sufferings, knowing that suffering produces endurance, and endurance produces character, and character produces hope, and hope does not disappoint us, because God's love has been poured into our hearts through the Holy Spirit who has been given to us. (Rom. 5:1–5)

> Of this gospel I was made a minister according to the gift of God's grace which was given me by the working of his power. To me, though I am the very least of all the saints, this grace was given, to preach to the Gentiles the unsearchable riches of Christ, and to make all men see what is the plan of the mystery hidden for ages in God who created all things; that through the church the manifold wisdom of God might now be made known to the principalities and powers in the heavenly places. This was according to the eternal purpose which he has realized in Christ Jesus our Lord, in whom we have boldness and confidence of access through our faith in him. So I ask you not to lose heart over what I am suffering for you, which is your glory. For this reason I bow my knees before the Father, from whom every family in heaven and on earth is named. (Eph. 3:7–14)

> This is evidence of the righteous judgment of God, that you may be made worthy of the kingdom of God, for which you are suffering. (2 Thess. 1:5)

Do not be ashamed then of testifying to our Lord, nor of me his prisoner, but take your share of suffering for the gospel in the power of God. . . (2 Tim. 1:8)

On behalf of this man I will boast, but on my own behalf I will not boast, except of my weaknesses. Though if I wish to boast, I shall not be a fool, for I shall be speaking the truth. But I refrain from it, so that no one may think more of me than he sees in me or hears from me. And to keep me from being too elated by the abundance of revelations, a thorn was given me in the flesh, a messenger of Satan, to harass me, to keep me from being too elated. Three times I besought the Lord about this, that it should leave me; but he said to me, "My grace is sufficient for you, for my power is made perfect in weakness." I will all the more gladly boast of my weaknesses, that the power of Christ may rest upon me. For the sake of Christ, then, I am content with weaknesses, insults, hardships, persecutions, and calamities; for when I am weak, then I am strong. (2 Cor. 12:5–10)

Now I rejoice in my sufferings for your sake, and in my flesh I complete what is lacking in Christ's afflictions for the sake of his body, that is, the church. . . (Col. 1:24)

As can be seen through this strong testimony of St. Paul, suffering can be understood as a gift from God when it is accepted in a spirit of faithfulness and offered up for our own sins, as well as for the sins of others. Through suffering we find the intersection, the paradox, of the horizontal dimension of the Cross (representing Christ's self-emptying, weakness, and humiliation) and the vertical dimension of the Cross (representing Christ being lifted up, manifesting his power and glory). Only because of the sublime truth contained in these reflections one can conclude, "And for this reason suffering also has a special value in the eyes of the Church. It is something good, before which the

Church bows down in reverence with all the depth of her faith in the Redemption. She likewise bows down with all the depth of that faith with which she embraces within herself the inexpressible mystery of the Body of Christ."[28]

The Resurrection

Christianity does not begin with the death of Jesus, but rather with His glorious Resurrection from the dead, for the simple reason that if Jesus had not risen from the dead, then everything He taught and did would have been insignificant.[29] Through the Resurrection, Jesus definitively validates His claim of divinity, that He indeed is "the resurrection and the life,"[30] and it concretely expresses His victory over sin and even death itself. Indeed "The Resurrection of Jesus is the crowning truth of our faith in Christ, a faith believed and lived as the central truth by the first Christian community; handed on as fundamental by Tradition; established by the documents of the New Testament; and preached as an essential part of the Paschal mystery along with the cross" (CCC 638).

The strongest biblical passages we find concerning the importance of the Resurrection are found in Paul's first letter to the Corinthians, of which the entire fifteenth chapter is devoted to the theme of the Resurrection. Paul forcefully states:

> Now if Christ is preached as raised from the dead, how can some of you say that there is no resurrection of the dead? But if there is no resurrection of the dead, then Christ has not been raised; if Christ has not been raised, then our preaching is in vain and your faith is in vain. We are even found to be misrepresenting God, because we testified of God that he raised Christ, whom he did not raise if it is true that the dead are not raised. For if the dead are not raised, then Christ has not been raised. If Christ has not been raised, your faith is futile and you are still in your sins. Then those also who have fallen asleep in Christ have perished. If for this life only we have hoped in Christ, we are of all men most to be pitied. (1 Cor. 15:12–19)

---

28 Ibid., no. 24.
29 See CCC 651.
30 See John 11:25.

Relating back to the theme of redemptive suffering, recall that Jesus, in His risen and glorified body, still retained the wounds of His passion.[31] Why would that be? To signal to us that it is only through suffering and the acceptance of our own crosses that we can hope to rise with Christ. The risen Lord now bears the wounds of His Passion not in disgrace, but as a permanent testament to His victory over sin and death, and as a reminder of His constant plea before the Father on our behalf.[32]

For a period of forty days following His Resurrection, Jesus taught His apostles the fullness of what they had learned prior to His death,[33] and prepared them for the coming of the Holy Spirit at Pentecost,[34] who would lead them in all truth through the end of time. When the forty days were completed, Jesus ascended into heaven, body and soul, and thereby made heaven capable of receiving a glorified, human body. Ten days after the Ascension, the promised gift of the Holy Spirit[35] was outpoured upon the early Christians,[36] signaling the birthday of the Church and the completion of the Paschal Mystery.[37]

Conclusion

The primary Christological heresies that threatened the early Church have been briefly examined and their errors demonstrated. Contrary to the Docetists, we affirm that the Second Person of the Trinity truly became man; against the Adoptionists, we maintain that Jesus is the true Son of the Father; contra the Arians, we uphold the true divinity of Jesus, who is consubstantial with the Father; countering the Apollinarianists, we avow that Jesus had a rational human soul; in response to the Nestorians, we assert that there is one single divine subject in Jesus Christ; opposing the Monophysites, we proclaim the dual natures of Jesus Christ; and refuting the Monothelitites, we defend the truth of the two wills in the person of the Incarnate Son.

---

31 See John 20:24–29.
32 See St. Thomas Aquinas, *Summa Theologica* (Westminster, 1948), IIIa Q. 54 a.4.
33 See Luke 24:27.
34 See Acts 2:1–4. Pentecost is considered the "birthday" of the Church.
35 See Luke 24:49.
36 See Acts 2.
37 See CCC 1076. The Paschal Mystery refers to the life, death and Resurrection of Jesus.

The work of our redemption was already announced by God in the *protoevangelium* of Genesis[38] and preceded according to God's design. Jesus actively sacrificed Himself for all of us, so that we may have eternal life, and on the path to heaven we will inescapably experience suffering. Looking to Jesus as the pioneer of our faith, we are able to understand the role of suffering in the Christian life as it prepares us for our own Resurrection at the end of time.

---

38 The *protoevangelium* refers to the "first announcement of the Good News;" it is the first promise of salvation concerning the coming of the Messiah, and it is found in Genesis 3:15.

Chapter 9

Mariology

Overview

One of the most misunderstood areas of Catholic theology is mariology. One extreme view of Mary is that she is a goddess, equal to God Himself, and that devotion to her is seen as a substitute to authentic worship of almighty God. The other extreme maintains that Mary is no better than any other holy woman of the Bible, and therefore she should not be treated with greater reverence than any other important woman of salvation history. As we shall see, Catholic teaching on Mary rejects these two extremes, and in every case whatsoever, authentic Marian devotion is always centered on Jesus Christ, as stated by Pope Paul VI:

> In the Virgin Mary everything is relative to Christ and dependent upon Him. It was with a view to Christ that God the Father from all eternity chose her to be the all-holy Mother and adorned her with gifts of the Spirit granted to no one else. Certainly genuine Christian piety has never failed to highlight the indissoluble link and essential relationship of the Virgin to the divine Savior.[1]

---

1   Pope Paul VI, Apostolic Exhortation on the Right Ordering and Development of Devotion to the Blessed Virgin Mary *Marialis cultus*, no. 25.

The Four Marian Dogmas

A dogma is a solemnly proclaimed teaching of the faith. "Dogmas are lights along the path of faith; they illuminate it and make it secure" (CCC 89). There have been four defined dogmas concerning Mary: her Divine Maternity; her Immaculate Conception; her Perpetual Virginity; and her Bodily Assumption into heaven. We shall take a closer look at each one of these teachings.

MARY'S DIVINE MATERNITY

O God, who through the fruitful virginity of Blessed Mary bestowed on the human race the grace of eternal salvation, grant, we pray, that we may experience the intercession of her, through whom we were found worthy to receive the author of life, Our Lord Jesus Christ, your Son.

—Collect of the Liturgy for the
Solemnity of Mary, the Holy Mother of God

Of all the dogmas about Mary, the truth of Mary's divine motherhood is the most important, since if Mary were not the mother of God, then there would be no need for the other dogmas to apply. This dogma also explicitly reveals a perennial truth: authentic Marian teaching will always serve to safeguard the truth about Jesus Christ. This dogma of Mary's divine maternity did not so much affirm a truth about Mary as it did about Jesus.

In the 5th century, the patriarch of Constantinople named Nestorius insisted that the Son of God and the Son of Mary were two separate persons. This understanding of Nestorius rejects the truth that Jesus Christ is both the Son of God and the Son of Mary, a single divine person who united Himself to two natures.

Perhaps we can understand Nestorius' difficulty. When a woman gives birth, she brings into the world a new person who never existed before his or her conception. If we call Mary the Mother of God, then it would seem that we are really saying that prior to Jesus' conception, He as God did not exist, which would mean He could not be God! Nestorius neglected to consider that a woman gives birth to a person and not to a nature alone; the nature is always united to the person, and there is only one person in Jesus Christ.

To settle the matter, the Council of Ephesus was called in 431 and taught that Mary truly bore the Second Person of the Blessed Trinity and gave Him a true human nature. Therefore, Mary is rightly called the *Theotokos*, the Mother of God, but a few distinctions must be made. Mary gave a true human nature to God in conceiving Him and bearing Him, but she did not author His divine personhood, nor did she author His divine nature. From all eternity, the Logos existed as a divine person with a divine nature, but at His conception in the womb of Mary, He took on real human flesh and blood from His mother. Mary did give birth to the divine person of Jesus Christ, but she did not bring into being a new person, which is what happens with every other conception.

MARY'S IMMACULATE CONCEPTION

O God, who by the Immaculate Conception of the Blessed Virgin prepared a worthy dwelling for your Son, grant, we pray, that, as you preserved her from every stain by virtue of the Death of your Son, which you foresaw, so, through her intercession, we, too, may be cleansed and admitted to your presence.

—Collect of the Liturgy for the
Immaculate Conception of the Blessed Virgin Mary

Pope Pius IX solemnly defined the dogma of Mary's Immaculate Conception on Dec 8, 1854. This dogma teaches that Mary was conceived without original sin through no merit of her own, but through the intervention of almighty God in view of her role in salvation history.

Under normal circumstances in our world plagued with original sin, when two spouses have sexual relations and conceive a child, that newly-created child exists in a condition devoid of God's sanctifying grace. The newly-conceived child is good, but not holy. Through a singular privilege, meaning that this scenario is not true of any other human person in history, at the moment when Mary was conceived in her mother's womb, Mary never contracted a fallen nature, never inherited the condition nor the effects of original sin, and remained eminently holy her entire life.

Consider the following example: Before we sit down to eat dinner, we make sure we have clean hands so that our food does not become dirty. Before we go to Mass, we likewise make sure our hands are clean and we do not eat or drink anything[2] for at least one hour before receiving Holy Communion so that we are clean within as we prepare to receive our Lord. When the priest prepares to celebrate Mass, he makes sure the sacred vessels are clean and pure because they will contain the Body and Blood of the Lord. In a similar manner, God chose to come into the world through the spotless womb of Mary, a pure tabernacle untainted with the defilement of sin.

This dogma goes further than teaching that Mary was simply free from original sin; it also includes that Mary remained free from every actual sin during her entire lifetime. This teaching means that Mary never once in her life chose to sin against God: "By the grace of God Mary remained free of every personal sin her whole life long" (CCC 493).[3] This is why Mary is greeted by the angel Gabriel with the words, "Hail, full of grace" (Lk. 1:28). It is unfortunate that several biblical translations weaken this passage to read, "Hail, favored one." Many women in salvation history may be described as being "favored" by God, but Mary alone received the "fullness" or plenitude of grace. Mary alone was full of grace from the moment of her conception until the end of her life, resulting in a complete state of mutual opposition between her and the devil, as already foretold in Genesis in God's judgment of the serpent: "I will put enmity between you and the woman. . ." (Gen. 3:15). Mary is "the woman" who brings forth the promised Messiah who will indeed crush the head of the ancient serpent.

If Mary were free from original sin, and if Mary were free from all actual sin throughout her life, did Mary really need to be redeemed by Jesus Christ? The answer is an emphatic yes! Mary did not conceive herself; Mary did not remain free from all sin on her own merits without supernatural grace. God indeed redeemed Mary, since every human person after Adam needs to face the truth of original sin. In Mary's case, God directly redeemed her from the moment of her conception,

---

2 Except water or necessary medication.
3 See also Pope Pius XII, Encyclical Letter on the Mystical Body of Christ *Mystici corporis*, no. 110.

rather than redeeming her later in her life. When we are baptized, we appropriate the graces of the redemption into our own lives; however, for Mary, her sanctification took place at the moment of conception in such a way that she never received the fallen nature that we all possess.

A last component of the Church's teaching about the Immaculate Conception is that because Mary did not receive original sin, she also remained free from all the effects of original sin. Mary's intellect was never darkened in knowing the truth, meaning that Mary would have had the most perfect intellect of any human person in existence, comparable to that of Eve's before she sinned. Mary also had a will that was not weakened in any way, but always directed to the will of God: "Behold, I am the handmaid of the Lord; let it be to me according to your word" (Lk. 1:38). Mary was also completely free from concupiscence; although she was tempted by the devil throughout her life, she never had temptations to sin coming from within her, since her intellect and will were always united to God's will. Finally, Mary would not necessarily need to die. We shall return to this last point when we discuss the Assumption.

MARY'S PERPETUAL VIRGINITY

The Church teaches that Mary's perpetual virginity encompassed three phases: Mary was a virgin *prior* to the birth of Jesus; Mary was a virgin *during* the birth of Jesus; and Mary remained a virgin *after* the birth of Jesus.[4]

All Christians acknowledge Mary's virginity before the birth of Jesus, because the Bible clearly teaches it. For example, we read "When Joseph woke from sleep, he did as the angel of the Lord commanded him; he took his wife, but knew her not until she had borne a son; and he called his name Jesus" (Mt. 1:24–25) and "Mary said to the angel, 'How can this be, because I know not man'" (Lk. 1:34, Douay). In biblical idiom, the expression "to know" here refers to sexual intimacy, and these passages clearly illustrate that Mary had no sexual relations with Joseph prior to the conception of Jesus.

---

4   See the teaching of the Lateran Council of 649 presided over by Pope St. Martin I, Denzinger 256.

In discussing the conception of Jesus, it is important that we clarify a common error that persists among some Catholics to this day. We read in Matthew 1:18 that Mary and Joseph were betrothed when Mary conceived Jesus in her womb, and it is very common to compare the betrothed state of New Testament times with something akin to the state of two people being engaged today. The common understanding tends to be that Mary and Joseph were not married when Jesus was conceived, but simply engaged.

This position may seem acceptable on the surface, but it quickly breaks down: If Mary and Joseph, whom the Church upholds as the greatest model of family life, were simply engaged when Jesus was conceived, then what kind of example is God giving to us about marriage and family life? After all, if Jesus was conceived outside of wedlock, then why does the Church see non-married persons having sexual relations as a grave sin, on occasion causing psychological harm as well?

It is erroneous to claim that Mary and Joseph were merely engaged at the time of Jesus' conception. Betrothal, as understood at this time, was actually the first stage of the marriage; it marked the legal, solemn establishment of marriage. Once two persons were betrothed, the betrothal could only be broken through the issuance of a decree of divorce. Additionally, unfaithfulness to one's betrothed could bring the penalty of death, since it falls under the heading of marital unfaithfulness for the Jewish people. Finally, consider that Joseph is called the "husband" of Mary,[5] and one cannot speak of "husband" unless one is also speaking of "wife" and not mere "fiancée."

The second phase of Mary's perpetual virginity is her virginity during the birth of Jesus Christ. This means that Mary's bodily integrity, that is, the physical sign of her virginity, was preserved intact even in the act of birth itself, so that the baby Jesus would have "transported" out of her womb. As the Church teaches, the birth of Jesus "did not diminish his mother's virginal integrity but sanctified it."[6] The Fathers use the following example: Just as light passes through glass without causing the least damage or diminishment to the glass, so too did the

5 See Matthew 1:19.
6 Second Vatican Council, *Lumen gentium*, no. 57.

baby Jesus pass through his mother's womb without causing the least damage or diminishment to Mary's virginal integrity. As a result of this, Mary did not suffer labor pains in giving birth to Jesus. However, recalling the prophetic words of Simeon who told Mary "a sword will pierce through your own soul" (Lk. 2:35), it is true that Mary later suffered her spiritual labor pains at the foot of the Cross, when she gave birth to all of us as Mother of the Church through her cooperation with Jesus' redemptive work.

Some persons may raise the following objection: If Jesus did not really pass through Mary's birth canal (i.e. being born in a normal manner), then we can't say that Mary truly gave birth to Jesus. To this objection, we respond that there is no necessary connection between literally passing through the birth canal and the act of being born. Do we accuse mothers who have children delivered via a C-Section of "not truly giving birth" since the baby "did not pass through the birth canal"? Of course not. In the same way, the fact that Jesus did not pass through Mary's birth canal in the normal way in no way impugns the truth of her truly being the Mother of God.

The final phase of Mary's perpetual virginity is the phase that most (but not all) non-Catholic Christians reject, namely, that Mary never had sexual relations with Joseph (or anyone else) after Jesus was born. One common objection to this teaching appeals to Matthew 1:25, which reads, "he [Joseph] took his wife, but knew her not until she had borne a son. . ." The implication seems to be that Joseph had sexual relations with Mary after the birth of Jesus.

In reply, we note that the Greek term translated as "till" (*heos*) means "up until that point" and does not refer to anything beyond the referenced time. For example, the same Greek term (*heos*) is used in the Septuagint for 2 Samuel 6:23, "And Michal the daughter of Saul had no child till (*heos*) the day of her death" (KJV). Are we to suppose that Michal had children after the day of her death? Certainly not! Consider as well the passage from 1 Corinthians 15:25, "For he must reign until he has put all his enemies under his feet." Are we to consider that once Jesus definitively conquers Satan at his Second Coming, then he will no longer reign as King over heaven and earth? Of course not! These examples are sufficient in showing that a proper interpretation of Matthew 1:25 cannot successfully be invoked to argue against the dogma of Mary's perpetual virginity.

A second objection to Mary's perpetual virginity may be suggested through Jesus' identification as the "first born" son of Mary.[7] If Jesus is the "first" born, then it seems logical that there must be others born after him. This thinking fails to take into account the understanding of what "first born" meant in Jewish society. There were special obligations on the part of the parents concerning the birth of their first born, and the position of the first born in Jewish society was above that of any other siblings (with few exceptions accomplished through divine intervention). Consequently, a son would consider himself a firstborn irrespective of whether other brothers existed after him.

The most common objection against Mary's perpetual virginity concerns the "the brothers of the Lord"[8] mentioned in the New Testament. To this objection, the Catechism states,

> Against this doctrine the objection is sometimes raised that the Bible mentions brothers and sisters of Jesus. The Church has always understood these passages as not referring to other children of the Virgin Mary. In fact James and Joseph, "brothers of Jesus", are the sons of another Mary, a disciple of Christ, whom St. Matthew significantly calls "the other Mary." They are close relations of Jesus, according to an Old Testament expression. (500)

Just as the term "brother" is today used in various cultural backdrops, in biblical times it could denote bonds of kinship due to extended family ties (such as cousins), or common affinity (such as being of the same ethnicity or religion). The constant teaching of the Fathers and Doctors of the Church is that Mary remained a virgin, a teaching that is also strongly held by Eastern Orthodox Christians.

---

7   See Luke 2:7, and some translations of Matthew 1:25.
8   See Mark 6:3.

Mary's Assumption into Heavenly Glory

O God, who, looking on the lowliness of the Blessed Virgin Mary, raised her to this grace, that your Only Begotten Son was born of her according to the flesh and that she was crowned this day with surpassing glory, grant through her prayers, that, saved by the mystery of your redemption, we may merit to be exalted by you on high.

—Collect of the Liturgy for the
Assumption of the Blessed Virgin Mary

Proclaimed by Pope Pius XII on November 1, 1950, the dogma of Mary's Assumption declares, "The Immaculate Mother of God, the ever-virgin Mary, having completed the course of her earthly life, was assumed body and soul into heavenly glory."[9] Through this event, Mary was preserved from bodily corruption, and her body was glorified immediately, instead of waiting until the Second Coming.

> [I]t seems impossible to think of her, the one who conceived Christ, brought him forth, nursed him with her milk, held him in her arms, and clasped him to her breast, as being apart from him in body, even though not in soul, after this earthly life. Since our Redeemer is the Son of Mary, he could not do otherwise, as the perfect observer of God's law, than to honor, not only his eternal Father, but also his most beloved Mother. And, since it was within his power to grant her this great honor, to preserve her from the corruption of the tomb, we must believe that he really acted in this way.[10]

It may be surprising to consider that no one really knows whether or not Mary died. There are two opinions on the matter, both of which are theologically acceptable. The majority position, represented by those who believed that Mary died, is called the mortalist position. This position maintains that Mary experienced death, the temporary

---

9   Pope Pius XII, Apostolic Constitution on The Most Bountiful God: Defining the Dogma of the Assumption *Munificentissimus Deus,* no. 44.
10   Ibid., no. 38.

separation of the soul from the body, yet not long enough for her body to undergo corruption. This perspective is the most widely held, and is even referenced (without being stated) several time in Pope Pius XII's dogmatic proclamation. This view has also been supported by Pope John Paul II, who remarked:

> Some theologians have in fact maintained that the Blessed Virgin did not die and was immediately raised from earthly life to heavenly glory. However, this opinion was unknown until the 17th century, whereas a common tradition actually exists which sees Mary's death as her entry into heavenly glory. Could Mary of Nazareth have experienced the drama of death in her own flesh? Reflecting on Mary's destiny and her relationship with her divine Son, it seems legitimate to answer in the affirmative: since Christ died, it would be difficult to maintain the contrary for his Mother.[11]

The minority position, represented by those who believe that Mary did not die, is known as the immortalist position. The logic of this position is that since Mary did not inherit original sin, nor ever sin in her life, she would not have died, since death is a punishment for sin.

The theological opinion of Pope John Paul II and the weight of the tradition notwithstanding, either of these positions is theoretically acceptable, as long as the position is not maintained for the wrong reason. For example, one cannot maintain that Mary died because she is a sinner like everyone else, nor could someone maintain that Mary did not die because she is a goddess. So while it is important to stress the likelihood that Mary did indeed die, one may safely speculate that she might have transitioned from this life to heavenly glory without experiencing the temporary separation of soul and body brought about through death. This being said, the weight of the argument seems to favor Mary's death.

---

11 Pope John Paul II, General Audience of June 25, 1997.

The Rosary

One of the most misunderstood prayers in Catholicism is the Rosary, a vocal and meditative prayer that focuses on the mysteries of the life of Jesus. The complete Rosary has twenty mysteries, five from each group of Joyful, Luminous, Sorrowful, and Glorious. The Rosary is essentially a Christological prayer, evident through the fact that 90 percent of its mysteries directly pertain to the life of Jesus Christ. It is also a thoroughly scriptural prayer, since its key prayers[12] all directly flow from the Bible. As to its great benefit for the Christian life, Pope Paul VI wrote, "As the history of the Church makes clear, this very fruitful way of praying is not only efficacious in warding off evils and preventing calamities, but is also of great help in fostering Christian life"[13]

The Joyful Mysteries are: 1) The Annunciation to Mary that she has been chosen to be the mother of God; 2) The Visitation of Mary to her cousin, Elizabeth, who was pregnant with John the Baptist; 3) The Nativity of Jesus Christ; 4) The Presentation of Jesus in the Temple as the firstborn of Mary forty days after his birth, and 5) The Finding of Jesus in the Temple when he was twelve years old.

The Luminous Mysteries are: 1) The Baptism of Jesus in the Jordan River when he was thirty years old by John the Baptist; 2) The Miracle of the Wedding Feast at Cana, which was the first of Jesus' public miracles; 3) The Proclamation of the Kingdom of God; 4) The Transfiguration of Jesus; and 5) The Institution of the Sacrament of the Eucharist at the Last Supper.

The Sorrowful Mysteries are: 1) The Agony of Jesus in the Garden of Gethsemane the night before He died; 2) The Scourging of Jesus at the Pillar with barbaric whips that had hooks and small ball bearings at the end to rip the flesh; 3) The Crowning of Jesus with Thorns; 4) Jesus Carrying His Cross from Pilate's palace to Calvary; and 5) The Crucifixion and death of Jesus for our sins.

The Glorious Mysteries are: 1) The Resurrection of Jesus three days after His death; 2) The Ascension of Jesus into heaven, body and soul, forty days after His Resurrection; 3) The Descent of the Holy Spirit

---

12 The "Hail Mary," "Our Father," and the "Glory Be."
13 Pope Paul VI, Encyclical Letter on Prayers for Peace *Christi matri*, no. 10.

upon the apostles and holy women ten days after the Ascension; 4) The Assumption of Mary into Heaven, body and soul; and 5) The Coronation of Mary as queen of heaven and earth.

Although the Rosary in its current form underwent centuries of development, and mindful that even today Catholics living in various countries throughout the world pray the Rosary a bit differently with respect to the introductory prayers and manner in which each mystery is announced, its origin stems back to St. Dominic (13th century), the founder of the Dominican order. According to tradition, he was given the Rosary by the Virgin Mary as a spiritual weapon to combat heresy, and to this day the praying of the Rosary has been highly encouraged by popes and saints alike.

Conclusion

The four defined Marian dogmas: Mary's Divine Maternity; Immaculate Conception; Perpetual Virginity; and Assumption into heavenly glory not only teach us the full truth about Mary who is "placed by the grace of God, as God's Mother, next to her Son, and exalted above all angels and men,"[14] but also leads us deeper as we grow in love for her Son, the one mediator between God and man.[15] The Rosary is the most well-known Catholic prayer, and is a beautiful expression of Christian piety that seeks deeper union with Jesus through Mary.

---

14 Second Vatican Council, *Lumen gentium*, no. 66.

15 Consider the following excerpt from the Second Vatican Council: "There is but one Mediator as we know from the words of the apostle, 'for there is one God and one mediator of God and men, the man Christ Jesus, who gave himself a redemption for all.' The maternal duty of Mary toward men in no wise obscures or diminishes this unique mediation of Christ, but rather shows his power. For all the salvific influence of the Blessed Virgin on men originates, not from some inner necessity, but from the divine pleasure. It flows forth from the superabundance of the merits of Christ, rests on his mediation, depends entirely on it and draws all its power from it. In no way does it impede, but rather does it foster the immediate union of the faithful with Christ" (*Lumen gentium*, no. 60).

Chapter 10

Eschatology

Overview

In this last chapter we shall turn our attention to eschatology, which is the branch of theology that focuses upon the "last things" that take place beginning with our bodily death. We shall probe the concepts of judgment, purgatory and the doctrine of indulgences, hell, and heaven.

The following words of C.S. Lewis call to mind the two choices ultimately faced by every human person, and the influence we may have on the path others may choose:

> It is a serious thing to live in a society of possible gods and goddesses, to remember that the dullest and most uninteresting person you can talk to may one day be a creature which, if you say it now, you would be strongly tempted to worship, or else a horror and a corruption such as you now meet, if at all, only in a nightmare. All day long we are, in some degree, helping each other to one or other of these destinations.[1]

As Lewis points out, the ultimate landscape of eternity will consist of the righteous whom will shine like the sun in a perfect state of holiness emulating the eternal Son,[2] and the damned who are perpetually

---

1   C.S. Lewis, *The Weight of Glory* (New York: HarperCollins, 2001), 45–46.
2   See Matthew 13:43.

consumed with pride and hatred. There will be no middle way, no common ground between these two diametrically opposite, possible conclusions to each and every human life, with the final outcome resting in our own hands. When we go before God for judgment, there will be no surprises. He simply confirms and brings to pass the judgment that we have already brought upon ourselves according to how well we have dedicated our lives to both love of God and love of neighbor.

Judgment

There are two judgments that take place after our death. The first is Particular Judgment, sometimes also called Individual Judgment, and it takes place immediately upon the final separation of our soul from our earthly body. The second judgment is called the Last Judgment, or the General Judgment, or the Final Judgment, and it differs from Particular Judgment in several ways.

Whereas Particular Judgment takes place immediately upon death,[3] the Last Judgment will not take place until the end of the world, at which time every human being will appear before God.[4] The Church teaches,

> The Last Judgment will come when Christ returns in glory. Only the Father knows the day and the hour; only he determines the moment of its coming. Then through his Son Jesus Christ he will pronounce the final word on all history. (CCC 1040)

Additionally, unlike Particular Judgment, the Last Judgment will not simply concern our souls but at this time our souls will finally be reunited with our bodies, as we profess in the Creed "I believe in the Resurrection of the Body." No mere metaphor is employed here: "The 'resurrection of the flesh' (the literal formulation of the Apostles' Creed) means not only that the immortal soul will live on after death, but that even our 'mortal body' will come to life again" (CCC 990, referencing Rom. 8:11). The bodies of all the saints will be glorified, as expressed in the beauty of Dante: "When our flesh, made glorious

---

3 See CCC 1021 and 1022.
4 See CCC 998 and 1001.

at the Judgment Seat, dresses us once again, then shall our persons become more pleasing in being more complete."[5]

At the time of the Last Judgment, purgatory will cease to exist, and all the souls who were previously in the state of purgatory and who have not yet entered heaven will be granted entrance into heaven. The Last Judgment cannot alter the outcome of Particular Judgment, and therefore persons who are sent to either heaven or hell upon their death will remain there forever. The Last Judgment, in addition to being the occasion for the final unification of the body with the soul, is a public, universal witness to God's ultimate triumph over the forces of sin and death.

Purgatory

Earlier in this book, it was pointed out that to enter into heaven upon death, a person must be free from mortal sin and be in a state of sanctifying grace. While it is correct to maintain that anyone who dies in the state of sanctifying grace is *assured* heaven, it would be incorrect to maintain that the only pre-requisite for *entrance* into heaven is being in the state of sanctifying grace. In order to enter into God's abode, which is a state of unsurpassed peace, happiness, purity, and love, one must be entirely free from every sin,[6] as well as all attachment[7] to created things. It would seem that very few people die in such a condition. Those who die in God's grace, but without being truly perfect, enter into the condition known as purgatory.[8] Purgatory is not a "second chance" for those who die in a state of wickedness, but rather an opportunity for

---

5   *The Divine Comedy*, canto XIV, 43–45.

6   Consider Revelation 21:22–27 in reference to the heavenly Jerusalem: "And I saw no temple in the city, for its temple is the Lord God the Almighty and the Lamb. And the city has no need of sun or moon to shine upon it, for the glory of God is its light, and its lamp is the Lamb. By its light shall the nations walk; and the kings of the earth shall bring their glory into it, and its gates shall never be shut by day—and there shall be no night there; they shall bring into it the glory and the honor of the nations. *But nothing unclean shall enter it*, nor any one who practices abomination or falsehood, but only those who are written in the Lamb's book of life" (emphasis added).

7   It is reasonable and normal to enjoy and make use of created things in moderation, but we must never become attached to such things; we must be prepared to do without our "creature comforts" for the sake of a greater good.

8   See CCC 1030.

those who die already in a state of imperfect holiness to achieve full holiness.[9]

Purgatory is sometimes called "the mercy of God," because without it, only those relatively few persons who die in a state of perfection could ever hope to enter heaven. Purgatory is the condition existing after death of a person being purified from any unforgiven venial sins, as well as the way by which reparation for sins already forgiven can still be made. Jesus set the bar quite high—he did not tell us simply to live a "good" life, or even a predominately "holy" life, but he told us to be *perfect*, as recorded in the central moral teaching of the Sermon on the Mount: "You, therefore, must be perfect, as your heavenly father is perfect" (Mt. 5:48). While it is true that no human can live in a state of moral perfection relying solely upon one's own power, it is equally true that, by cooperating with God's grace, we can indeed attain moral perfection. God never commands the impossible, and he does command Christian perfection. It will not come easily, nor will it come overnight, but if we trust in God and do our part, it will indeed come.

To restate the issue: a person who dies in the state of sanctifying grace, but who has committed unforgiven venial sins, or who dies without sin, but has not yet fully made reparation for sins already forgiven, would enter into the condition of purgatory immediately upon death. While it is true that the Sacrament of Confession forgives sins, it does not necessarily satisfy the reparation that still must be made.[10] For this reason, a person who dies immediately after making a good confession would certainly be assured entrance into heaven, but most likely not until the person has endured purgatory for a time, in order to make reparation for those sins that have already been forgiven.

---

9   "It is necessary to explain that the state of purification is not a prolongation of the earthly condition, almost as if after death one were given another possibility to change one's destiny. The Church's teaching in this regard is unequivocal and was reaffirmed by the Second Vatican Council which teaches: 'Since we know neither the day nor the hour, we should follow the advice of the Lord and watch constantly so that, when the single course of our earthly life is completed (cf. Heb. 9:27), we may merit to enter with him into the marriage feast and be numbered among the blessed, and not, like the wicked and slothful servants, be ordered to depart into the eternal fire, into the outer darkness where 'men will weep and gnash their teeth' (Mt. 22:13 and 25:30)" (*Lumen gentium*, n. 48). Pope John Paul II, General Audience of August 4, 1999.

10 See CCC 1473.

The sin is immediately forgiven through sacramental absolution, but the reparation to be made goes beyond the absolution:

> For the forgiveness of sins committed after Baptism, this process is centered on the sacrament of Penance, but it continues after the sacramental celebration. The person must be gradually "healed" of the negative effects which sin has caused in him (what the theological tradition calls the "punishments" and "remains" of sin). At first sight, to speak of punishment after sacramental forgiveness might seem inconsistent. The Old Testament, however, shows us how normal it is to undergo reparative punishment after forgiveness. God, after describing himself as "a God merciful and gracious . . . forgiving iniquity and transgression and sin," adds: "yet not without punishing" (Ex. 34:6–7). In the Second Book of Samuel, King David's humble confession after his grave sin obtains God's forgiveness (cf. 2 Sam. 12:13), but not the prevention of the foretold chastisement (cf. ibid., 12:11; 16:21). God's fatherly love does not rule out punishment, even if the latter must always be understood as part of a merciful justice that re-establishes the violated order for the sake of man's own good (cf. Heb. 12:4–11).[11]

To better understand the distinction between the sin and the reparation that must be made to correct the injustice that entered the world through that sin, consider the following example. Suppose a student takes a course and at the end of the semester, receives a failing grade. The student then decides, in his anger and frustration, to throw a brick through the window of the professor's house. The next day the student rings the doorbell of the professor's home and confesses to the professor that he broke the window, explaining that he is truly sorry for his impetuous behavior and asks if he can be forgiven. The professor's response, "Yes, I forgive you" does not bring closure to the story; the

11 Pope John Paul II, General Audience of September 29, 1999, nos. 2–3.

127

student is not yet free to go on his merry way. Although he has been forgiven, the problem of the broken window still remains; the student is responsible for having it repaired. Only when the window is fixed is the situation fully settled. The same is true with the spiritual life. It is necessary for us to seek forgiveness for our sins, but it is insufficient to stop at the level of forgiveness. We must proceed to make reparation, to fix the moral disorder we introduced into the world through our sin.

Although not explicit, the concept of purgatory can be found within Sacred Scripture. For example, consider the following excerpts:

> Now if any one builds on the foundation with gold, silver, precious stones, wood, hay, stubble—each man's work will become manifest; for the Day will disclose it, because it will be revealed with fire, and the fire will test what sort of work each one has done. If the work which any man has built on the foundation survives, he will receive a reward. If any man's work is burned up, he will suffer loss, though he himself will be saved, but only as through fire. (1 Cor. 3:12–15)

> Therefore I tell you, every sin and blasphemy will be forgiven men, but the blasphemy against the Spirit will not be forgiven. And whoever says a word against the Son of man will be forgiven; but whoever speaks against the Holy Spirit will not be forgiven, either in this age or in the age to come. (Mt. 12:31–32)

The first passage from St. Paul uses the imagery of precious metal and stones to denote our virtuous deeds and the imagery of wood, hay and straw to refer to our base deeds. The "Day" of the Lord refers to His coming in judgment, at which time we receive a "trial by fire" that polishes and adds further radiance to the precious metals and stones, but destroys all evil. Given the presence of the precious metal, the person is in the grace of God, but not yet perfect since there is also a fair share of material that needs to be burned away. The fire that will save that person, taking away the bad and further polishing the good, is the condition of purgatory.

With respect to the second passage from the Gospel of Matthew, Pope St. Gregory the Great interprets it as applying to purgatory, since the passage admits of the possibility of some sins—but not the sin of blasphemy against the Holy Spirit—being forgiven in the next life."[12]

We, the living, are able to intercede for the souls of the faithful departed, as indicated in 2 Maccabees 12:45, "Therefore he made atonement for the dead, that they might be delivered from their sin." This intercession is possible because the faithful on earth, those in heaven, and those in the intermediate state of purgatory all comprise the Communion of Saints. As Pope Benedict XVI states,

> The souls of the departed can, however, receive "solace and refreshment" through the Eucharist, prayer and almsgiving. The belief that love can reach into the afterlife, that reciprocal giving and receiving is possible, in which our affection for one another continues beyond the limits of death—this has been a fundamental conviction of Christianity throughout the ages and it remains a source of comfort today. Who would not feel the need to convey to their departed loved ones a sign of kindness, a gesture of gratitude or even a request for pardon?[13]

We also find in the Church's understanding of indulgences specific ways to completely satisfy the reparation needed for sins already forgiven, whether for ourselves or the souls in purgatory.

Indulgences

An indulgence is defined as "a remission before God for the temporal punishment for sins, whose guilt is forgiven, which a properly disposed member of the Christian faithful obtains under certain and clearly defined conditions through the intervention of the Church, which, as the minister of Redemption, dispenses and applies authoritatively the treasury of the expiatory works of Christ and the saints."[14] And it may be

---

12 See CCC 1031.

13 Pope Benedict XVI, Encyclical Letter on Christian Hope *Spe salvi*, no. 48.

14 The Apostolic Penitentiary, *Manual of Indulgences* (Washington DC: USCCB Publishing, 2006), no. 1.

gained either for oneself or for a deceased person,[15] but not for another living person. Indulgences are classified as either "partial" or "plenary." A partial indulgence remits "part" of the temporal punishment[16] due to sin, whereas a plenary indulgence remits all temporal punishment due to sin.

Should a person die in the state of grace and without any further remission of temporal punishment needed, that person would immediately gain entrance to heaven. Important to note, however, is that a plenary indulgence remits all temporal punishment for sins already committed; it does not extend into the future, and should one continue sinning, the need for the remission of temporal punishment due to those new sins is still needed.

Only baptized members of the Church who are in the state of sanctifying grace by the completion of the prescribed work, and who have the general intention of gaining an indulgence, are actually able to do so,[17] and only one plenary indulgence may be granted per day. The Church's authority to regulate indulgences is based in the power of the keys given by Jesus to Peter as recorded in Matthew 16:13–20, specifically, the power to "bind and loose" sins, both on earth and in heaven.

There are four conditions that the Church requires for granting a plenary indulgence. These conditions are going to Confession; receiving the Holy Eucharist; praying for the intentions of the Pope; and having the interior disposition of complete detachment from all sin, even venial sin. This last requirement is by far the most difficult, and should any of these conditions not be fulfilled, and should the

---

15 "We should recall that no man is an island, entire of itself. Our lives are involved with one another, through innumerable interactions they are linked together. No one lives alone. No one sins alone. No one is saved alone. The lives of others continually spill over into mine: in what I think, say, do and achieve. And conversely, my life spills over into that of others: for better and for worse. So my prayer for another is not something extraneous to that person, something external, not even after death" (Pope Benedict XVI, *Spe salvi*, no, 48).

16 "Temporal punishment" is contrasted with "eternal punishment." Whereas mortal sin brings with it eternal punishment, venial sin brings with it temporal punishment. Once a mortal sin is confessed, the eternal punishment is remitted, although the temporal punishment still remains. See CCC 1472–1473.

17 *Manual of Indulgences*, no. 17 §1–2.

person be seeking a plenary indulgence, then that indulgence would become partial.[18]

There has been much speculation about the timeframe in which the above conditions must be satisfied in relation to the completion of the indulgenced work, since the Church simply states, "the three conditions[19] may be fulfilled several days before or after the performance of the prescribed work; it is, however, fitting that Communion be received and the prayer for the intention of the Holy Father be said on the same day the work is performed."[20] An authoritative answer can be found in the following document by the Vatican's Apostolic Penitentiary:

> It is appropriate, but not necessary, that the sacramental Confession and especially Holy Communion and the prayer for the Pope's intentions take place on the same day that the indulgenced work is performed; but *it is sufficient that these sacred rites and prayers be carried out within several days (about 20) before or after the indulgenced act.* Prayer for the Pope's intentions is left to the choice of the faithful, but an "Our Father" and a "Hail Mary" are suggested. One sacramental Confession suffices for several plenary indulgences, but a separate Holy Communion and a separate prayer for the Holy Father's intentions are required for each plenary indulgence.[21]

Some examples of works for which a plenary indulgence may be gained include: adoration of the Blessed Sacrament for at least thirty minutes; devout reading of the Bible for at least thirty minutes; and recitation of the Rosary (five decades) in a church or with members of the family. A fuller list of indulgenced works, as well as a more extended

---

18 Although the practice of granting indulgences has historically been abused at times within the Church (for example, in 16th century Europe), it is important to note that the Church does not "sell" indulgences (as is sometimes claimed by non-Catholics), and one cannot "buy" his or her way into heaven.

19 Confession, Eucharist, and prayer for the Pope's intentions.

20 *Manual of Indulgences,* no. 20 §2.

21 Cardinal William Wakefield Baum, "The Gift of the Indulgence," given in Rome at the offices of the Apostolic Penitentiary, January 19, 2000, emphasis added.

treatment of the Church's doctrine of indulgences may be found in the *Manual of Indulgences* (Washington, DC: USCCB Publishing, 2006).

Hell

God is a God of love, and therefore He wills the salvation of all people,[22] as St. Paul teaches in Scripture, "[God] desires all men to be saved and to come to the knowledge of the truth" (1 Tim. 2:4). Yet God is also perfectly just, and for those who freely choose eternal exile from God, "the teaching of the Church affirms the existence of hell and its eternity. Immediately after death the souls of those who die in a state of mortal sin descend into hell, where they suffer the punishments of hell, 'eternal fire'" (CCC 1035). A number of misinformed Catholics think that hell is a myth; that Satan is imaginary; that there is no such thing as "eternal damnation." The Church has never disavowed these truths, nor could she, because they are firmly grounded both in Sacred Scripture and Sacred Tradition. Perhaps the most well-known eschatological biblical passage affirming the existence of hell is found in the Gospel of Matthew:

> When the Son of man comes in his glory, and all the angels with him, then he will sit on his glorious throne. Before him will be gathered all the nations, and he will separate them one from another as a shepherd separates the sheep from the goats, and he will place the sheep at his right hand, but the goats at the left. Then the King will say to those at his right hand, "Come, O blessed of my Father, inherit the kingdom prepared for you from the foundation of the world. . . ." Then he will say to those at his left hand, "Depart from me, you cursed, into the eternal fire prepared for the devil and his angels. . . ." And they will go away into eternal punishment, but the righteous into eternal life. (Mt. 25:31–34; 41, 46)

Like heaven, hell is forever, so those who go to hell upon death will never be released from it. The question may arise, "But how could a

22 See CCC 1037.

loving God keep a soul in hell, even when the person decides to repent and seek forgiveness?" In response, it must be noted that there can be no more decisions made after death that could change one's spiritual orientation at the moment of death. If a person dies in a state of unrepentant mortal sin, that person will never have the desire to repent after death. Neither fallen angels (demons, such as the devil), nor humans in hell will ever desire to repent, and therefore hell is forever.

Heaven

"Heaven is the ultimate end and fulfillment of the deepest human longings, the state of supreme, definitive happiness" (CCC 1024). In the New Testament, we find the image of a wedding feast used to describe the joys of heaven,[23] and it becomes evident that the degrees of happiness attained in heaven will not be the same for all persons. Passages like "For he will render to every man according to his works" (Rom. 2:6) and "In my Father's house are many rooms" (Jn. 14:2) support the understanding that although everyone in heaven will be perfectly happy, some persons will have a greater share in God's glory than others. For example, Mary, the Mother of God, shares in more glory than any other angel or saint, since she followed the teachings of her Son in a deeper and greater way than any other created being, and whose personal relationship to the person of Christ is unrivaled in the created order.

An analogy may be helpful to better understand how we can speak of universal perfection in heaven, yet varying degrees of how intimately each saint shares in the life of God. Imagine that we have a shot glass, a water bottle, and a bucket sitting on the desk. All of them are filled with water to the point that each respective container cannot hold any more, yet the bucket contains a greater quantity of water than the water bottle, which contains a greater quantity of water than the shot glass. We are all vessels of the Lord waiting to be filled, however some persons can hold more of God's spiritual gifts than others.

Entrance into heaven marks the salvation of the individual, which is our ultimate goal, a goal that can only be obtained through the Church. Consider the following teaching of the Second Vatican Council:

---

23 See Matthew 22:2; 25:1–13.

This Sacred Council wishes to turn its attention firstly to the Catholic faithful. Basing itself upon Sacred Scripture and Tradition, it teaches that the Church, now sojourning on earth as an exile, is necessary for salvation. Christ, present to us in His Body, which is the Church, is the one Mediator and the unique way of salvation. In explicit terms He Himself affirmed the necessity of faith and baptism and thereby affirmed also the necessity of the Church, for through baptism as through a door men enter the Church. Whosoever, therefore, knowing that the Catholic Church was made necessary by Christ, would refuse to enter or to remain in it, could not be saved.[24]

The Council clearly teaches that outside the Church there is no salvation; however, the Council goes on to point out that there are various ways by which one can be incorporated into the Church. It is true that Catholics are the most fully incorporated into the Church, yet all people of good will are in differing ways partially incorporated into the one Church of Christ, to the extent that the Council states,

Those also can attain to salvation who through no fault of their own do not know the Gospel of Christ or his Church, yet sincerely seek God and moved by grace strive by their deeds to do his will as it is known to them through the dictates of conscience. Nor does Divine Providence deny the helps necessary for salvation to those who, without blame on their part, have not yet arrived at an explicit knowledge of God and with His grace strive to live a good life.[25]

To summarize: Those who may know that the Catholic Church is necessary for salvation, and refuse to become visible members of the Church as Catholics, cannot be saved. But those who do not realize in conscience that the Catholic Church is necessary for salvation, and

---

24 Second Vatican Council, *Lumen gentium*, no. 14.
25 Ibid., no. 16.

yet do their best to live a holy life, are considered to be imperfectly incorporated into the Church, and therefore may still be saved through it by Jesus Christ. If a person is saved, that person is saved only by Jesus Christ, and it is the will of Jesus Christ to save people only through the Church that He founded upon Peter, as the Catechism reminds us: "Salvation comes from God alone; but because we receive the life of faith through the Church, she is our mother" (169; cf. Mt. 16:18). Ignorance of this fact, through no fault of a person, will not hinder that person's salvation.

Conclusion

Heaven is our true home, and yet hell remains a possibility for each one of us. It is fully our choice as to what will become of us after our death through the way we live now on earth. In His abundant mercy, God offers purgatory to His faithful ones who have died in His love, but who are not yet spiritually prepared to enter into heavenly glory. Through the ministry of the Church, God also avails to us indulgences as means to make reparation for our sins before our death, or to assist the faithful departed to finally enter into heavenly glory.

⁂
Selected Bibliography

Aquinas, Thomas. *Summa Theologica*, trans. Fathers of the English Dominican Province. 5 volumes. New York: Benziger Brothers, Inc., 1948.

Aumann, Jordan. *Christian Spirituality in the Catholic Tradition*. San Francisco: Ignatius Press, 1985.

Baum, William Wakefield. "The Gift of the Indulgence." January 19, 2000.

Benedict XVI. Apostolic letter *Porta fidei*. October 11, 2011.

——— *Jesus of Nazareth: From the Baptism in the Jordan to the Transfiguration*. New York: Doubleday, 2007.

——— "Saint Athanasius of Alexandria." General Audience, June 20, 2007.

——— "Saint Augustine of Hippo, Part I." General Audience, January 09, 2008.

——— "Saint Augustine of Hippo, Part IV." General Audience, February 20, 2008.

——— "Saint Augustine of Hippo, Part V." General Audience, February 27, 2008.

——— "Saint Basil, Part I." General Audience, August 01, 2008.

——— "Saint Gregory of Nyssa, Part II." General Audience, September 5, 2007.

——— "Saint Gregory the Great, Part II." General Audience, June 04, 2008

——— "Saint Gregory Nazianzus." General Audience, August 08, 2008.

——— "Saint Gregory Nazianzus, Part II." General Audience, August 22, 2008.

——— "Saint Jerome." General Audience, November 07, 2007.

——— "Saint Jerome, Part II." General Audience, November 14, 2007.

——— "Saint John Chrysostom, Part I." General Audience, September 19, 2007.

——— *Spe salvi*. November 30, 2007.

——— *Verbum Domini*. September 30, 2010.

Catechism of the Catholic Church, Second Edition. Washington, D.C.: United States Catholic Conference—Libreria Editrice Vaticana, 1997

Denzinger, Heinrich. *Compendium of Creeds, Definitions, and Declarations on Matters of Faith and Morals*, trans. Peter Hünermann. San Francisco: Ignatius Press, 2012.

Dziwisz, Stanislaw. *A Life with Karol*. New York: Doubleday, 2007.

Flannery, Austin (ed). *The Documents of Vatican II, Volume 1: The Conciliar and Post Conciliar Documents*. New York: Costello Publishers, 1996.

Gaul, Cyril. *Rome and the Study of Sacred Scripture*. Indiana: Abbey Press, 1964.

John Paul II. *Dives in misericordia*. November 13, 1980.

———— *Fidei depositum*, October 11, 1992.

———— *Fides et ratio*, September 14, 1998.

———— *On the Gift of Indulgences*. General Audience, September 29, 1999.

———— *Ordinatio sacerdotalis*. May 22, 1994.

———— *Reconciliatio et paenitentia*. December 2, 1984.

———— *Salvifici doloris*. February 11, 1984.

Leo XIII. *Providentissimus Deus*, November 18 1893.

Lewis, Clive Staples. *The Weight of Glory*. New York: HarperCollins, 2001.

Paul VI. *Christi matri*. September 15, 1966.

———— *Marialis cultus*. February 2, 1974.

———— *Sedula cura*. June 27, 1971.

Pius X. *Praestantia Sacrae Scripturae*. November 18, 1907.

Pius XII. *Divino afflante spiritu*, September 30, 1943.

———— *Humani generis*. August 12, 1950.

———— *Muntificentissimus Deus*. November 1, 1950.

———— *Mystici corporis*. June 29, 1943.

Ratzinger, Joseph. *Called to Communion*. San Francisco: Ignatius, 1996.

———— *The Spirit of the Liturgy*. San Francisco: Ignatius, 2000.

Schaff, Philip (ed). *The Nicene and Post-Nicene Fathers*. Edinburgh: T. & T. Clark, Series I and II, 29 vols.

United States Conference of Catholic Bishops. *Manual of Indulgences*. Washington D.C., 2006.

Weigel, George. *Witness to Hope*. New York: Harper Perennial, 2005.

CPSIA information can be obtained
at www.ICGtesting.com
Printed in the USA
FSHW01n2304090518
47842FS

9 781937 155988